Five Years' Explorations At Thebes: A Record Of Work Done 1907-1911...

George Edward Stanhope Molyneux Herbert Carnarvon (Earl of), Howard Carter, Anonymous, Anonymous

This work has been selected by scholars as being culturally important, and is part of the knowledge base of civilization as we know it. This work was reproduced from the original artifact, and remains as true to the original work as possible. Therefore, you will see the original copyright references, library stamps (as most of these works have been housed in our most important libraries around the world), and other notations in the work.

This work is in the public domain in the United States of America, and possibly other nations. Within the United States, you may freely copy and distribute this work, as no entity (individual or corporate) has a copyright on the body of the work.

As a reproduction of a historical artifact, this work may contain missing or blurred pages, poor pictures, errant marks, etc. Scholars believe, and we concur, that this work is important enough to be preserved, reproduced, and made generally available to the public. We appreciate your support of the preservation process, and thank you for being an important part of keeping this knowledge alive and relevant.

FIVE YEARS'
EXPLORATIONS AT THEBES

OXFORD
PLATES AND LETTERPRESS
PRINTED AT THE UNIVERSITY PRESS
BY HORACE HART

ELECTRUM STATUETTE OF A YOUTH
XVIIIᵀᴴ DYNASTY: PERIOD OF AMENHETEP I

FIVE YEARS' EXPLORATIONS AT THEBES

A RECORD OF WORK DONE 1907–1911

BY
THE EARL OF CARNARVON [George Edward Stanhope Molyneux Herbert, 5th]
AND
HOWARD CARTER

WITH CHAPTERS BY
F. LL. GRIFFITH, GEORGE LEGRAIN, GEORGE MÖLLER
PERCY E. NEWBERRY AND WILHELM SPIEGELBERG

WITH SEVENTY-NINE PLATES AND FRONTISPIECE

HENRY FROWDE
OXFORD UNIVERSITY PRESS
LONDON, NEW YORK, TORONTO AND MELBOURNE
1912

N5350
.C319
(RECAP)

PREFACE

THE following volume contains a record of work done in the Theban Necropolis during the years 1907-11. In the editing of this report I have availed myself of the generous help of several scholars, whose names appear at the heads of the chapters they have contributed. To these gentlemen I wish to tender my sincere thanks for their co-operation.

Mr. Howard Carter has been in charge of all operations; and whatever successes have resulted from our labours are due to his unremitting watchfulness and care in systematically recording, drawing, and photographing everything as it came to light.

To Professor Sir Gaston Maspero, the Director-General of the Service des Antiquités, I wish to proffer my thanks for his most kind and valuable support; as also to Mr. Weigall, who, in the course of his official work, has given me his most willing assistance. To Dr. Budge I should also like to express my indebtedness for several valuable suggestions.

CARNARVON.

HIGHCLERE,
    August 1911.

CONTENTS

	PAGE
PREFACE. By the Earl of Carnarvon	v
INTRODUCTION. By the Earl of Carnarvon	1
Chapter I The Mortuary Chapel and Sepulchre of Teta-Ky. By Howard Carter	12
II The Paintings and Inscriptions of the Vaulted Chamber of Teta-Ky. By George Legrain	14
III The Funerary Statuettes from Tomb of Teta-Ky. By Percy E. Newberry	19
IV Excavations in the Valley of Dêr el Bahari. By Howard Carter	22
V Work done in the Birâbi. The Seventeenth Dynasty Tomb No. 9. By Howard Carter	34
VI The Carnarvon Tablets I and II. By F. Ll. Griffith	36
VII The 'Valley'-Temple of Queen Hatshepsût. By Howard Carter	38
VIII Ptolemaic Vaulted Graves. By Howard Carter	42
IX Demotic Papyri and Ostraca. By Wilhelm Spiegelberg	46
X Colonnade and Foundation Deposit of Rameses IV. By Howard Carter	48
XI Other Antiquities discovered. By Howard Carter	49
XII The Late Middle Kingdom and Intermediate Period Necropolis. By Howard Carter	51
XIII Hieratic Texts from Tomb No. 37. By George Möller	89
XIV The Vegetable Remains. By Percy E. Newberry	94
INDEX	95
ILLUSTRATIONS: PLATES I–LXXIX	At end

ILLUSTRATIONS

FRONTISPIECE

ELECTRUM STATUETTE OF A YOUTH: XVIIIth DYNASTY
PERIOD OF AMENHETEP I

FIGURES IN TEXT

FIG.		PAGE
1.	Excavations in the Birâbi	2
2.	First Appearance of the 'Valley'-Temple Wall	3
3.	The 'Valley'-Temple Wall	5
4.	Tomb No. 25	6
5.	Tomb No. 37	7
6.	Uninscribed Cones of the Eleventh Dynasty	8
7.	Votive Cake-offering—Tomb of Kha-em-hat	9
8.	Chert Chisels and Hammers	10
9.	Scarab from Tomb No. 5	27
10.	Hieratic Inscriptions from 'Valley'-Temple	39
11.	Graffiti on Stones from 'Valley'-Temple	40
12.	Gilt Copper Vessel from Ptolemaic Vaulted Graves	43
13.	Ptolemaic Coins from Ptolemaic Vaulted Graves	44
14.	Key to Gaming-board	57

ILLUSTRATIONS

LIST OF PLATES AT END

PLATES I–XII: TOMB OF TETA·KY:

I   (1) Open Court-yard; (2) Vaulted Chambers.
II Plan of Tomb.
III (1) Right Wall of Painted Niche; (2) Left Wall of Painted Niche.
IV (1) Ceiling Decoration; (2) Ceiling Decoration and Frieze.
V   Scenes on North Wall.
VI Scenes on Eastern and Western Walls.
VII–IX Scenes on Southern Wall.
X   (1) Shawabti Figure in Model Coffin; (2) Shawabti Figure of Sen-senb.
XI Model Coffins.
XII (1) Table for Offerings; (2) Funerary Statuettes.

PLATES XIII–XXIV: DÊR EL BAHARI VALLEY:

XIII   Panoramic View showing the Sites excavated.
XIV   Tomb No. 5 before and after opening.
XV   Plan of Tomb No. 5.
XVI   Series of Coffins from Tomb No. 5.
XVII   Tomb No. 5, Antiquities from.
XVIII   Tomb No. 4, Limestone Statuette; and Pottery from Tombs Nos. 1–16.
XIX   (1) Foundations of Wall of Amenhetep I and Aahmes-nefert-ari;
        (2) Offerings to a Tree.
XX   (1) Serpentine Wall; (2) Bathing Slab.
XXI   (1) Offerings from Dromos Deposit; (2) Brick-lined Hole for Dromos Deposit.
XXII   Dromos Deposit. (1) Pottery and (2) Implements.
XXIII   (1) Child's Toy; (2) Pottery from Excavations; (3) Stamped Bricks of Amenhetep I and Aahmes-nefert-ari.
XXIV   Panoramic View showing Site of 'Valley'-Temple and of Dromos Deposits.

LIST OF ILLUSTRATIONS

PLATES XXV–XXIX: TOMB No. 9:

- XXV (1) Three sides of a Canopic Box; (2) Three Canopic Jars in Pottery.
- XXVI Types of Pottery.
- XXVII Carnarvon Tablet I, *obverse*.
- XXVIII Carnarvon Tablet I, *reverse*.
- XXIX Carnarvon Tablet II, *obverse* and *reverse*.

PLATES XXX–XXXII: HATSHEPSÛT'S 'VALLEY'-TEMPLE:

- XXX Plan of Hatshepsût's 'Valley'-Temple and Neighbouring Tombs.
- XXXI Northern Boundary Wall of 'Valley'-Temple.
- XXXII (1) Tally-stone of Hatshepsût; (2) Stamped Brick of Hatshepsût; (3) Wooden Hoe; (4) Stamped Bricks of Hatshepsût and Thothmes I.

PLATES XXXIII–XXXIX: PTOLEMAIC VAULTED GRAVES:

- XXXIII View of Ptolemaic Vaulted Graves over Site No. 14.
- XXXIV (1) Amphorae beneath Floor of Vaulted Grave; (2) Façade of Vaulted Grave.
- XXXV } Carnarvon Papyrus I.
- XXXVI
- XXXVII Demotic Dockets and Inscribed Potsherd.
- XXXVIII } Carnarvon Papyrus II.
- XXXIX

PLATE XL: SITE No. 40:

- XL Foundation Deposit of Rameses IV.

PLATES XLI–XLIII: SITE No. 14:

- XLI A XXIInd Dynasty Stela.
- XLII (1) Osiride figure; (2) Mud Feretory or Shrine; (3) Reed Burial of a Man; (4) Inscriptions on Underside of Lid of a Box.
- XLIII Funerary Statuettes and Model Coffins.

PLATES XLIV–XLVII: TOMB No. 24:

- XLIV (1) Statuette of Ankhu; (2) Mummy Decoration; (3) Wooden Doll; (4 and 5) Faience Bowl.
- XLV (1) Jewel-box; (2) Contents of Jewel-box; (3) Scribe's Palette.
- XLVI (1) Jewel-box; (2) Contents of Jewel-box.
- XLVII Pottery Vessels and Pans.

LIST OF ILLUSTRATIONS

PLATES XLVIII–LII: TOMB No. 25:

XLVIII   (1) Ivory and Ebony Toilet-box ; (2) the same with Drawer and Lid open.
XLIX   (1) Scene Engraved on Front of Toilet-box ; (2) Inscriptions on Lid of Toilet-box.
L   (1 and 2) Gaming-board and Playing Pieces in Ivory.
LI   (1) Blue Faience Hippopotamus ; (2) Necklace, Mirror, and Brooch.
LII   (1) Alabaster Toilet Vases ; (2) Pottery.

PLATE LIII: TOMBS Nos. 28, 29, 31, 32, 33, 34:

LIII   (1, 2, 5) Types of Pottery ; (3) *Rishi* Coffin (Tomb No. 32) ; (4) Dug-out Coffins (Tomb No. 29).

PLATE LIV: TOMBS Nos. 27 and 31:

LIV   Stela of the Keeper of the Bow, Auy-res.

PLATES LV–LXXVIII: TOMB No. 37:

LV   Plan of Tomb.
LVI   Central Passage showing Closed Doorway of Hall C.
LVII   North Wing of Corridor showing Closed Doorway of Chamber A.
LVIII   (1) Seal Impression on Doorway of Chamber A ; (2) Interior of Chamber A.
LIX   (1) Chamber B before Opening ; (2) Chamber B after Opening.
LX   (1) Decorated Rectangular Coffins ; (2) Plain Rectangular Coffins.
LXI   (1) Children's Coffins and Viscerae Boxes ; (2) Plain Anthropoid, 'Dug-out', and Semi-decorated Anthropoid Coffins.
LXII   (1) *Rishi* Coffins ; (2) Decorated Anthropoid Coffins of New Empire.
LXIII   Decorated Anthropoid Coffin of the New Empire.
LXIV   (1) Rush-work Baskets ; (2) Mechanical Toy Bird and Bird Trap.
LXV   (1) Toilet Set ; (2) Fan-holder, Kohl-pot, &c.
LXVI   Scribe's Outfit.
LXVII   (1) Electrum Statuette ; (2) Statuettes lying in Coffin No. 24 ; (3) Wooden Statuette.
LXVIII   (1) Objects from Decorated Rectangular Coffins ; (2) Objects from Plain Rectangular Coffins.
LXIX   (1) Objects from a Rectangular Gable-Topped Coffin ; (2) Objects from a Plain Rectangular Coffin.
LXX   Objects from *Rishi* Coffins.
LXXI   (1) Chair and Stool ; (2) Musical Instruments.
LXXII   Scarabs, Cowroids, and Rings.

LIST OF ILLUSTRATIONS

TOMB No. 37 (Continued).

    LXXIII   Bead Necklaces, Bangles, and Bracelet.
    LXXIV   Pottery Vessels.
    LXXV   Panel Stelae.
    LXXVI   (1 and 2) Writing Tablet No. 28, *reverse* and *obverse*; (3) Panel Stela.
    LXXVII   Writing Tablet No. 26, *obverse*.
    LXXVIII   Writing Tablet No. 26, *reverse*.

PLATE LXXIX: BOTANICAL SPECIMENS AND FIG BASKETS.

INTRODUCTION

BY THE EARL OF CARNARVON

The necropolis of Thebes—the great city which for so many centuries had been the capital of Egypt—lies on the western side of the Nile valley, on the margin of the desert opposite the modern village of Luxor. No ancient site has yielded a greater harvest of antiquities than this famous stretch of rocky land. From time immemorial it has been the profitable hunting-ground of the tomb robber; for more than a century a flourishing trade in its antiquities has been carried on by the natives of the district, and for nearly a hundred years archaeologists have been busy here with spade and pencil. The information that has been gleaned from its temple walls and tombs has enabled scholars to trace, point by point, the history of the city from at least 2500 B.C. to Ptolemaic times. The necropolis itself extends for some five miles along the desert edge, and evidences of the explorer and robber present themselves at every turn. Open or half-filled mummy pits, heaps of rubbish, great mounds of rock débris, with, here and there, fragments of coffins and shreds of linen mummy-wrappings protruding from the sand, show how active have been the tomb despoilers. Notwithstanding all the work that has been done here, very little can, in any sense, pretend to have been carried out in a systematic manner; and as few records of the various excavations have been kept, the work of the present-day explorer must necessarily be a heavy one. Often he will get no further in his excavations than the well-sorted-over dust of former explorers; and if he is fortunate enough to make a 'find', it is often only after clearing away a vast amount of rock débris and rubbish to the bed-rock below.

With a view to making systematic excavations in this famous necropolis, I began tentative digging among the Kurneh hills and desert margin in the spring of 1907. My workmen were all from the neighbouring villages and their number has varied from seventy-five to two hundred and seventy-five men and boys. I had three head reises—Mansûr Mohammed el Hashâsh, Mohammed Abd el Ghaffer, and Ali Hussên—who all worked well and satisfactorily. The labourers themselves were a willing and hard-working lot: but though they were no more dishonest than other Egyptian fellahin, inducements for them to steal were many, and we found it essential to proceed in our work with great care. I made it a rule that when a tomb was found, as few workmen as possible should be employed; and, in order that the opportunity for stealing should be reduced to a minimum, no clearing of a chamber or pit was carried on unless Mr. Carter or I was present. That nothing should escape us, we also, in certain cases, had to sift over the rubbish from the tombs three times.

My preliminary excavations eventually resulted in my confining attention to three sites in that part of the necropolis which lies between the dromos leading to Dêr el Bahari and the great gorge giving entrance to the valley of the Tombs of the Kings. These three sites were: (1) a spot a few metres to the north of the village mosque, where, according to the natives, lay a hidden tomb; (2) the Birâbi,[1] which is near the desert edge, between the hills of Drah abu 'l Nagga and

FIG. 1. EXCAVATIONS IN THE BIRÂBI.

the cultivated land, and adjoins the entrance to the dromos of Hatshepsût's famous terrace temple; and (3) that part of the XIth Dynasty cemetery which lies along the hill slope, on the northern side of the Dêr el Bahari valley.

Excavation on the first site was begun in 1908, and, after a fortnight's arduous work among the native houses and rubbish heaps of the village, an important inscribed tomb of the beginning of the XVIIIth Dynasty was opened. This tomb proved to be of a 'King's Son' named Teta-Ky, and contained, among many painted scenes, a figure of Aahmes-nefert-ari, the queen of Aahmes I and mother of Amenhetep I. This is the earliest known portrait of the celebrated queen, who

---

[1] *Birâbi* is the plural of *birba*, an 'ancient temple', but here the name is locally used more for a 'vaulted tomb', of which many occur in the district.

INTRODUCTION

afterwards became the patron goddess of the necropolis: she is figured as of fair complexion and not black, as is usually the case in her portraits of a later date. The scene shows her adoring the goddess Hathor, as a cow issuing from a cliff; and behind her is a lady, presumably the queen's mother,[1] named Teta-hemt, who is otherwise unknown. In the course of clearing this tomb many wooden Funerary Figures, in model coffins, were brought to light. These figures were of two types: (1) rudely carved mummiform figures with model coffins of wood,

Fig. 2. First Appearance of the 'Valley'-Temple Wall.

clay, or pottery, some of which were inscribed with hieratic or linear hieroglyphic texts; and (2) well-carved figures in wood, painted and with gilt faces, and inscribed with an early form of Chapter VI of the Book of the Dead. The figures of the first type were all found in the four niches in the courtyard wall

---

[1] Unfortunately the inscription above the lady is mutilated, but the personal name, Teta-hemt, is preceded by a ⌒ *t* and an —•— *s*. The *s*, as Professor Newberry has pointed out to me, must be the 3rd pers. sing. suffix *s* 'her', and he would suggest the restoration 🦉 ⌒ *mt-s*, 'her mother'. An alternative reading would be 𓇋 ⌒ *snt-s*, 'her sister', but the usual writing of this group is with ～ *n*: thus 𓇋⌒. 🦆 ⌒ *sat-s*, 'her daughter', is very improbable.

(Pls. 1 and II). Those of the second type were buried in pairs in shallow holes round the four sides of the top of the main pit shaft in the centre of the courtyard floor (Pl. II). The placing of shawabti figures in this position—as it were for them to guard the mouth of the pit of the sarcophagus chamber—is only known in this instance.

The clearance of Teta-Ky's tomb having been completed, we turned our attention to the Birâbi site. Three days' digging in the loose débris unmasked a hidden burial-place. Masses of pottery and denuded mummies were brought to light, and at the very threshold of the tomb (afterwards numbered 9) were discovered two wooden tablets (one in fragments) covered with stucco and inscribed with hieratic texts. One of these tablets has written (1) on its obverse, an important historical text relating to the expulsion of the Hyksos kings by the King Kamosi; and (2) on its reverse, a copy of part of the well-known Proverbs of Ptah-hetep.

In the early spring of 1909 work was continued on the Birâbi site. The tomb (No. 9), discovered the previous season, was finally cleared, but nothing further was found in it. Jutting out of one side of the hole caused by the excavation of the tomb, however, appeared the beginning of a well-built stone wall. About forty metres' length of this wall was cleared, and though unfinished, the masonry in general was good. A doorway, giving ingress from the north (see Plan, Pl. XXX), eighteen metres along its length, showed that its northern side formed its exterior face. The facing of the stone blocks, not agreeing in direction of their chiselling, showed that they had been re-used from some older building, and as the size of the blocks and their chiselling were similar to the masonry of the Mentu-hotep temple at Dêr el Bahari, it was conjectured that the wall must be of a date posterior to the XIth Dynasty. Regarding the purpose of the wall, we obtained no clue in 1909, nor could we then date it with any precision. In 1910, however, we found several blocks lying near the wall which bore hieratic inscriptions giving the name of Hatshepsût's master-builder, Pu-am-ra. Afterwards, similar inscriptions were found on the blocks built in the masonry. These, together with a single block bearing the name of the great queen's famous architect, Senmut, clearly proved that the wall which we had found must have belonged to some building of Hatshepsût's reign. Further clearance revealed that the building was of the nature of a terrace temple like that at Dêr el Bahari. So far as we can at present see, the axis of the building corresponds to the axis of the dromos leading to Hatshepsût's temple. This point, together with the fact that a foundation deposit with objects bearing the prenomen of the queen and the name of her temple (*Zeser-zeseru*) was brought to light, apparently in the centre of our monument, shows that we are dealing with a building in some way connected with the temple at Dêr el Bahari. The probable interpretation is that this newly-discovered 'Terrace Temple' is in reality a 'Valley'-Temple or 'Portal' to Hatshepsût's noble monument at Dêr el Bahari. It would, therefore, correspond to the so-called 'Valley'-Temples of Gizeh and Abusir. Another interesting fact relating to Hatshepsût's Dêr el Bahari temple was the discovery of a foundation deposit at the north-west corner of the

INTRODUCTION

dromos (Pl. XXIV, b), where it joins the temple. This is the largest deposit that has hitherto been discovered, and exhibits two new features in connexion with the custom of placing of such deposits, namely, the consecration of the building by unction and flesh and blood offerings. These offerings were kept separate from the usual model tools and implements which were found near by, and the vessels containing the unguents and wines were smashed, and their contents, as well as grains of corn, were poured over the clean sand that filled the cache. In 1911 search was made for the companion deposit in the south-west corner (Pl. XXIV, c); this was soon found, and it differed only in the fact that the secondary group— i. e. the tools and implements—was missing.

FIG. 3. THE 'VALLEY'-TEMPLE WALL.

Beneath the foundations of the 'Valley'-Temple we cut through a layer of rock débris averaging two metres in thickness, and discovered a series of pit and corridor tombs hewn in the rock-bed below. These had all been plundered, some indeed twice, and most of their contents had been scattered and some burnt. Several bore evidence of having been pilfered, in the first instance, shortly after the close of the Middle Kingdom, and then again during Hatshepsût's reign, probably by the workmen employed in building the 'Valley'-Temple. As evidence of the earlier plundering we may mention the fact that fragments of one stela were found in two separate tombs (Nos. 27 and 31), on opposite sides of the great wall. After this first plundering, the rock débris must have collected to a considerable depth above the tombs before the second spoliation took place, for rough retaining walls, built of stones and bricks found in the mounds, were made to support the sides of the shafts pierced through the earth by the later robbers.

6   INTRODUCTION

The tombs, as we have already noted, are of two types: (1) pit tombs, comprising a vertical shaft with one or more chambers at the bottom, and (2) corridor tombs, with open court in front, vestibule and passage leading to chambers with vertical shafts, and sarcophagus chamber below. In all cases the original

FIG. 4. TOMB No. 25.

contents had been plundered and some of the tombs had been re-used towards the end of the Intermediate period. One of the pit tombs, however, contained an unopened coffin and objects scattered about the chambers, which all clearly belonged to the original burial. Fortunately one of the objects—the fine casket figured in Pl. XLVIII—was inscribed with the cartouche of Amenemhat IV, and

INTRODUCTION

this enabled us to date with precision tomb No. 25. This casket is of ivory, ebony, and cedar wood, and was found broken into about two hundred pieces, which have been admirably fitted together, and the whole box restored to its original form by Mr. Carter. Beside the names of Amenemhat IV this casket bore the name of the 'Keeper of the department of Food', Kemen. It is interesting to note that in the prayer inscribed upon the top of the lid, the god invoked is Sebek, Lord of 𓎛𓈖𓏏 *Ḥent*, a locality in the Fayûm where the later XIIth Dynasty kings appear to have been very active. Among the objects found in this tomb and belonging to the same early date, were the board for a game, which Mr. Carter has succeeded in elucidating (p. 56), a coffin bearing the name of Ren-senb, and containing, besides the mummified body, a fine bronze mirror with ebony handle

FIG. 5. TOMB No. 37.

mounted in gold, and a beautiful necklace of gold-capped obsidian beads. In tomb No. 24 were necklaces of beads and amulets characteristic of the same period, and a mounted XIIth Dynasty scarab-seal. The stela, fragments of which were found in tombs Nos. 27 and 31, is of the XIIIth Dynasty, and to the same period may be ascribed several other objects found in these tombs. All these antiquities certainly belong to the original interments; and this enables us to date the whole group of tombs to the period covered by the end of the XIIth and perhaps the whole of the XIIIth Dynasty.[1] These Middle Kingdom tombs, we have already noted, had in some cases been re-used: this fact was brought to light in 1910, when we discovered fragments of several *Rishi* coffins in both the pit and corridor tombs. Coffins of this type are peculiar to the XVIIth and early XVIIIth Dynasties; so in

---

[1] Among this group are several tombs which may perhaps be referred to a slightly later date.

8 INTRODUCTION

them we had evidence of the tombs having been re-used at this period. In 1911 further light on this point was obtained by the discovery of tomb No. 37, which we found to contain some sixty-four coffins, and a large number of miscellaneous objects which may all be referred to the same period. Of the bricked-up chambers here, one bore seal impressions of Thothmes I, and among objects scattered over the floors of other chambers were scarabs of Amenhetep I, Thothmes I, Thothmes II, Hatshepsût, Neferu-ra, and Thothmes III, as well as several scarabs contemporary with the XIIIth Dynasty and the Hyksos period: the contents of this tomb thus cover the whole of the Intermediate period to the beginning of the reign of Thothmes III.

Altogether about 11,000 square metres of débris were cleared from the Birâbi site and, of course, many miscellaneous antiquities were brought to light in the

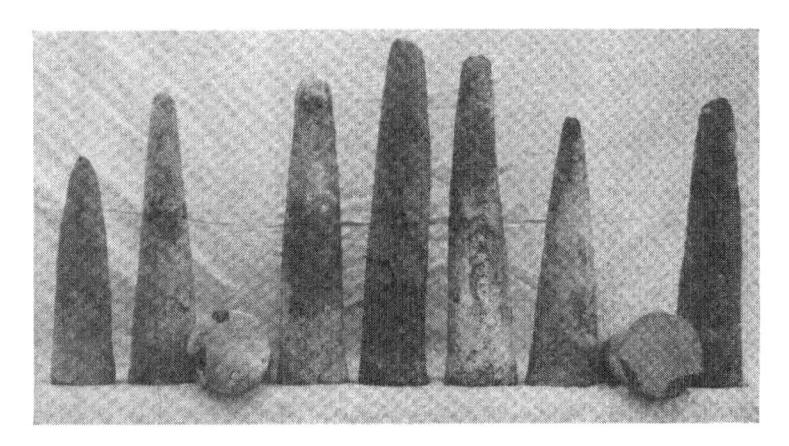

FIG. 6. UNINSCRIBED CONES OF THE XITH DYNASTY.

course of the excavation. On the débris and rubbish that had collected above the ruins of the 'Valley'-Temple were many vaulted graves, built of mud bricks; these, however, proved to have been plundered without exception. Under their floors were generally placed one or more amphorae which had been used for storing grain, water, and cakes, no doubt for the welfare of the deceased. One vase was sealed with clay and contained two well-preserved Demotic papyri, comprising deeds of sale, executed under Ptolemy Epiphanes; these documents, and a hoard of copper coins of Ptolemies III and IV, also found here, enable us to date the vaulted tombs to the Ptolemaic period.

Below these graves on the north-west corner of the site, and on the same level as the upper court of the 'Valley'-Temple, we unearthed paving slabs bearing marks of columns, with, beneath the corner of these substructures, a foundation

INTRODUCTION 9

deposit of Rameses IV. This, fortunately, enabled us to differentiate the building from the earlier temple; but we have as yet no further clue as to its nature, except that it was of stone quarried from the Dêr el Bahari temple of the Queen.[1]

The third site which we worked was along the northern slope between the north-eastern foot hills of the Dêr el Bahari valley and the Queen's temple.

FIG. 7. VOTIVE CAKE-OFFERING.

Along the face of the cliff here are the rock-cut tombs of the great nobles of the Early Middle Kingdom, and lower down are some graves of their retainers. These tombs had been re-used at the time of the Priest Kings, and were afterwards again violated. Then at a later period they were used for interments of Saite date, and, lastly, they served as dwelling-places for the Copts.

[1] This was demonstrated by the presence of stone chippings bearing fragments of the temple paintings that had been chipped off in refacing.

Out of the fifteen locations investigated by us only one (No. 5) gave any reward, and here we found undisturbed burials of a poorish class of people belonging to late Saite times.

In nearly all the early tombs pottery cones were found, sometimes in great numbers, but not in a single case did we obtain one that was inscribed. They were always found in the front courts and were certainly contemporary with the tombs of the Early Middle Kingdom. In all other parts of the Theban necropolis these cones date from the beginning of the New Empire[1] downwards, and, with rare exceptions, they have the names and titles of the deceased persons for whom they were made. Their real meaning has always been an open question. Maspero has suggested that they are model cakes or loaves of bread, made in burnt clay for the sake of permanency. Rhind found them built into a wall in a tomb court; and

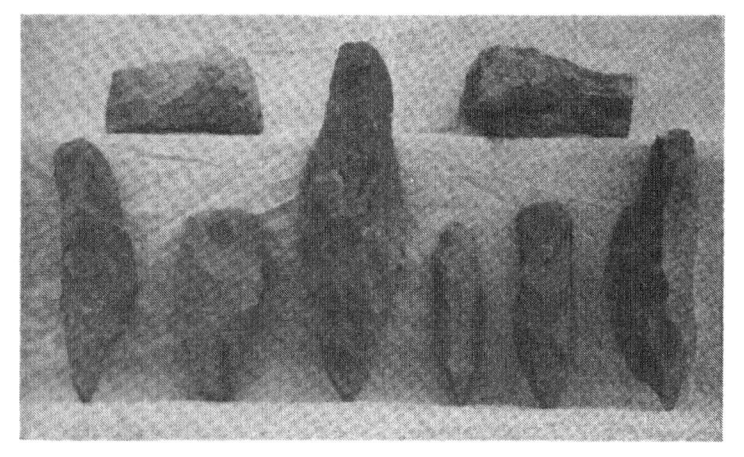

FIG. 8. CHERT CHISELS AND HAMMERS.

he and others have asserted that they were intended for ornament in the construction of the tombs. The same argument that they were meant for decoration might be used in the case of the pots that the modern natives frequently use when building light walls at the present day in the same tombs. The bas-relief in the tomb of Kha-em-hat, shown in Fig. 7, together with the fact that the cones are found nearly always on the floors of the open courtyard of tombs, tends to corroborate the theory of Maspero.

Distributed over the surface of the hillside were numbers of chert hammers and chisels, and also heaps of flakes, showing that they had been made on the spot. These are exactly similar to others that have been found at Beni Hasan and other

---

[1] The earliest inscribed specimens known bear the cartouches of Aahmes I.

rock-cut tomb sites of Egypt. They were probably used for the rougher work when hewing out the rock.

Our trenches near to the Dêr el Bahari temple exposed the workmen's dwellings and part of a large wall bearing the names, stamped upon its bricks, of Aahmes-nefert-ari and Amenhetep I. Here also were found votive offerings, as well as leaf offerings [1] in small pottery vessels, and oblations to trees.

These offerings to trees had already been noticed during the excavation of Hatshepsût's temple by the Egypt Exploration Fund,[2] when trees were discovered in the Lower Terrace with similar votive objects buried in the earth around them. In the tombs of the XVIIIth Dynasty and later periods representations of people offering to trees are often found; while even at the present day a general feature of the Mohammedan cemetery is its tree (generally a *gemmêz*, 'sycomore-fig'[3]), under which water and other offerings are often placed by mourners, while rags are attached to its branches or twigs. In the tomb of Thothmes III the deceased king himself is depicted[4] as receiving nourishment from the tree through a breast that protrudes from one of its boughs. It is interesting to note in regard to the votive offerings that within 600 yards of the scene of our excavations the tomb of Sheikh Abd El Kurneh, the local Mohammedan saint, is surrounded by heaps of mud model houses, small vessels of henna, and even the latest European wax candles, to invoke his assistance for the public weal.

[1] In Spiegelberg and Newberry's *Theban Necropolis* (p. 8) there is upon a stela a prayer which reads: 'May every one love him if he is spreading water upon the leaves before my stela.'
[2] Naville, *Archaeological Report*, 1894–5, p. 37.
[3] In India the Sacred Fig (*Ficus religiosa*) is venerated by the natives, who will not allow the tree to suffer mutilation or destruction.
[4] Loret, *Le tombeau de Thoutmes III*, Pl. 6.

CHAPTER I

THE MORTUARY CHAPEL AND SEPULCHRE OF TETA-KY

By Howard Carter

Though partly excavated in the rock at the side of a foot-hill the Mortuary Chapel of Teta-ky and his family is mainly a crude mud-brick construction, with its actual sepulchres subterranean: these latter are approached from a vertical shaft in the centre of the fore-court (Pl. I. 1 and 2).

The peculiar irregularity of the courtyard and buildings, which will be seen from the plan (Pl. II), seems due, in the first place, to the shape of the site, and, secondly, to the fact that this particular part of the necropolis must have been much overcrowded. Though it is built of mud-brick, the structure itself suffered comparatively little damage until recent years. The low walls of its fore-court, entered from the east, the small painted shrine in the south wall, the vaulted chambers on either side of the alley that leads to the principal and decorated chapel under the rock at the north end, are all more or less intact. In fact, the greater part of its destruction can be put down to the Arabs of modern times. Hence, except from slight mutilations, the structure is still practically intact.

Architecturally the plan and construction is of a well-known type. Its chapels are early examples of the brick-vaulted chambers often found in and so typical of the Dêr el Medînet Necropolis of Thebes. Only two of its chambers are painted: the small shrine or niche built in the wall of the fore-court; and the main chapel under the rock called upon the plan 'painted vaulted chamber'. The latter alone has inscriptions.

The painted niche has depicted on its right wall seated figures (unnamed) receiving offerings (Pl. III. 1); and on the left wall a conventionally drawn vineyard, in which there is shown a figure gathering grapes (Pl. III. 2). Its barrel-vaulted ceiling, now destroyed, was decorated with multicoloured bands which are so frequently seen on the roofs of Theban rock-cut tombs. But of this ceiling hardly enough remains to allow a true and accurate description.

The main chapel, or painted vaulted chamber, has upon its walls the usual funereal, husbandry, and offering scenes, and among the people portrayed are relatives of Teta-ky (see further description by Legrain, p. 14). Its segmental barrel-vaulted ceiling is painted, like the Beni Hasan tombs, with a wooden key-beam running longitudinally down the centre, painted yellow with darker and almost red graining (Pl. IV. 1); and on either side of the beam, above a *Kheker* frieze, the space is divided by black lines into red, yellow, and white squares (Pl. IV. 1 and 2). The red and white squares contain quatrefoils. In fact, to quote Professor Newberry's description[1] of the ceiling decoration of the tomb of Amenemhat would be to describe the roof ornamentation here, it differing only by the absence of imitation mat-work in the centre. Below the *Kheker* frieze is a band of hieroglyphic inscription giving the names of the deceased, and of his mother.

An interesting and new feature is the series of four small niches along the west wall of the open courtyard (Pl. I. 1 and Pl. II). In these niches were found numerous shawabti figures in model coffins of mud and wood (see further description by Newberry, p. 20). This I believe to be the only instance where such figures have actually been found *in situ*, a fact of some importance, for so little is known about the provenance of these early figures.

Another important discovery was eight similar, but more fully developed figures in wooden sarcophagi (see further description by Newberry, p. 19) placed in pairs on each of the four sides of the mouth of the shaft leading to the subterranean sepulchral chambers (Pl. II). These were buried about a foot below the surface, and were dedicated to persons buried in the vaults below. The reason for their being so placed is unknown; they were possibly guardian figures, like the magical ones placed in the walls of later tombs at the four cardinal points.[2]

From the north and east walls of the main painted chamber are two passages which could not be excavated further than the plan shows, owing to their being under modern native houses. But judging from the kind of rubbish that choked them they appear to have been opened and ransacked. This was probably done by tunnelling from the interior of the native houses above.

[1] Newberry, *Beni Hasan*, I, pp. 20, 29, 37.
[2] Carter and Newberry, *Tomb of Thoutmosis IV*, pp. 9, 10.

CHAPTER II

THE PAINTINGS AND INSCRIPTIONS OF THE PAINTED VAULTED CHAMBER OF TETA-KY

By George Legrain.

The following description of the paintings of the tomb of Teta-ky is taken from notes I made in 1909 when I visited Lord Carnarvon's excavations. The notes I made at that time were not then intended for publication. This fact will explain their briefness. The tomb of Teta-ky having unfortunately been mostly destroyed by natives since that date, the copy of the texts and pictures that I took on the occasion of my visit in 1909, together with Mr. Howard Carter's photographs, are the only remaining records of this tomb.

The funerary chamber is rectangular. The shorter walls lie east and west, whilst the longer sides face north and south. The roof is vaulted, barrel in form, and fairly regular. The ceiling is painted with a many-coloured chequer pattern; this decoration can be well seen in Plate IV. 1 and 2.

The decorations of the north and south walls consist of a long row of *Kheker*-ornaments. Beneath this row there is a line of detailed hieroglyphs, and beneath these again are scenes which run from left to right. These pictures were painted on stucco mixed without straw. This stucco has fallen away in several places, which has naturally caused the disappearance of many portions of the scenes represented in the tomb. Added to these accidents the tomb was re-used in ancient times, and part of the scenes were covered with an opaque lime-wash. Besides all these mutilations, breaches, and holes have very much spoilt this curious monument.

The general scheme of decoration can be described as follows:—

Northern Wall. Scenes of the private life of Teta-ky.

Eastern Wall. Queen Nefert-ari presenting offerings to the funerary Hathor Cow, 'Lady of Dendera'.

Southern Wall. Funerary procession. Funeral and arrival of Teta-ky in the Kingdom of Osiris.

Western Wall. Teta-ky in adoration before Osiris Khent-amenti. Beneath, funerary banquet and stela of Teta-ky.

This order is adopted in the following description.

PAINTINGS AND INSCRIPTIONS OF CHAMBER OF TETA-KY

North Wall. The following text is above the scenes: [hieroglyphs]

Scene A (Pl. V). The dead man [hieroglyphs], 'The Royal Son Teta-ky', is seated beneath a kiosk, of which three columns are visible. The polychrome capitals of these columns are in the shape of lotus buds. Around his neck Teta-ky wears a large necklace, and he has armlets on his arms and bracelets on his wrists. His wife [hieroglyphs], 'The Lady Senba', is seated at his side with left arm around him. Teta-ky is receiving grapes from a girl standing before him.

[hieroglyphs]

Behind the girl is a woman standing near the right-hand column.

[hieroglyphs]

Scene B (Pl. V). Two women stand before three seated men. By the side of the smaller woman there is a harp. The text relating to this woman reads:— [hieroglyphs] The taller woman places her hands towards the face of the first seated man. He holds her by the left wrist. Above this woman is the name [hieroglyphs]

Above the first man is [hieroglyphs]

Above the second man is [hieroglyphs]

Above the third man is [hieroglyphs]

Scene C. A woman opening a small box shows its contents to two squatting men.

Above the woman [hieroglyphs]

Above the first man [hieroglyphs]

Above the second man [hieroglyphs]

16   THE PAINTINGS AND INSCRIPTIONS OF THE

Nine women follow. Their names read :—

(1)   (2)   (3)   (4)   (5)   (6)   (7)   (8)   (9)

Scene D. Much of this scene is covered with whitewash. A woman brings a cup in one hand, whilst in the other she holds a red clay vase. A squatting woman beneath a tree is in front of her. To the right a man paddles.

Harnessed and loaded donkeys are seen here (Pl. V). To the right men unload the donkeys. Further on a man squats before a heap of grain . Originally there existed three horizontal lines of hieroglyphs, of which only the following signs remain :—

(1)
(2)
(3)

East Wall. The decorations of this wall are arranged in the following manner :—

The Solar Disk spreads its wings above the two scenes, A and B.

Scene A (Pl. VI). To the left is depicted the Cow Hathor, white with brown markings, the Solar Disk between her horns. She is . Before the Cow Goddess, Queen Nefert-ari holds a flaming censer. Nefert-ari is followed by .

In the left lower corner of this scene, below the Hathor Cow, two men and a woman are carrying offerings.

Scene B. This scene on the right side is practically destroyed, only the picture of the Hathor Cow is remaining.

South Wall. Scenes, sections A and B divided by the entrance door, are headed by the following inscription :—

PAINTED VAULTED CHAMBER OF TETA-KY

Scene A (Pl. VII). The mummy is seen under a canopied sledge. Two men opposite each other embrace the mummy. A woman fondles the feet, another the head. On the side of the canopy a long coiled snake forms the frieze. A man with arms hanging by his sides follows behind the sledge. He wears a wig, necklace, and a long tunic, and is following the funeral procession. The sledge itself is pulled by three men and two beasts. Between these men and animals and the sledge a man is shown pouring water upon the ground to facilitate the traction of the sledge. Above this man we read [hieroglyphs], and above each of the men :— [hieroglyphs], followed by a name obliterated.

The driver places his left hand on the hind-quarters of the cattle and with his right hand lifts a stick as if to strike.

Three men, wearing curious high and open-work head-dresses, come forward to meet the funeral procession and dance before it (Pl. VIII). Above these dancers the following hieroglyphs can be read :— [hieroglyphs].

Scene B (Pl. VIII). Beneath the funerary canopy the mummy is placed upright. The priest throws a few grains of incense into a censer which he presents to the mummy. The mummy is perhaps of the *Rîshi* or feather type; that is to say, of the kind of decoration used for the mummy cases of the Antefs, and of the people of Thebes who died before the beginning of the XVIIIth Dynasty. A number of coffins of the same and more elaborate type have since been found by Lord Carnarvon in the necropolis of the XIIth to XVIIIth Dynasties in the immediate neighbourhood of Teta-ky's tomb.

Scene C (Pl. IX). To the right of this scene, in a Naos, stands the Osiris Khent-amenti clad in white, wearing the Upper Egyptian crown, and holding the crook and flail. In front of him, from left to right, are, firstly, the plan of an habitation in which two of the *MW*-dancers are walking. Secondly, two obelisks in red granite. Thirdly, two trees covered with fruit. Fourthly, two rows of four shrines containing gods, goddesses, and funerary genii.

Scene D (Pl. IX). This scene, almost entirely destroyed, depicted the transport of the *Tekenu* to the necropolis. This person is wrapt in red cloth and is squatting on a sledge. At this spot much of the wall is broken away. We read the following legend in front of the *Tekenu* :— [hieroglyphs], while above him is [hieroglyphs].

The ceremonial continues to the right. Above the break in the wall is the sign [hieroglyph], then [hieroglyphs], and right at the end is figured a coffer or box ornamented with a lion's head, which is carried on the shoulders of the officiating priests. Before these personages is an inscription which reads :— [hieroglyphs].

18 PAINTINGS AND INSCRIPTIONS OF CHAMBER OF TETA-KY

West Wall (Pl. VI). The decorations on this wall are arranged in the following manner:—

A. in centre. Vertical line of text [hieroglyphs] [hieroglyphs].

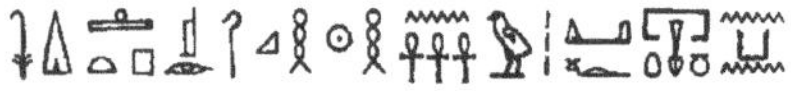

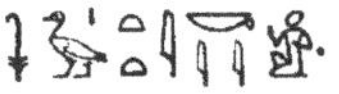

B. right side. The [hieroglyphs] presents numerous offerings piled upon an altar to Osiris Khent-amenti, who is seated upon a high pedestal and is clad in white and wears the Upper Egyptian crown. Behind Teta-ky the [hieroglyphs] cuts off the fore-leg of a white bull.

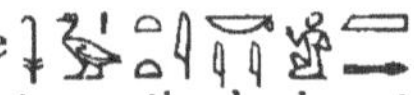

C. left side. The [hieroglyphs] stands before another similar Osiris Khent-amenti. He burns incense, pours water from a vase, and makes other oblations. Behind him a servant cuts off the fore-leg of a dark-coloured bull.

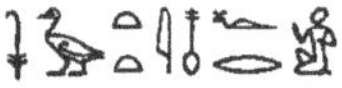

Lower portion.

D. Central false door. Almost entirely destroyed. Decorated with multi-coloured palm-leaf frieze; this was the funerary stela of Teta-ky.

E. Left side. On the left a man is seated. The text in this instance is so mutilated that his name [hieroglyphs] can alone be read. Behind him the lady [hieroglyphs] places her arms around his neck. In front of these two people, to the right, a man makes offerings and libations.

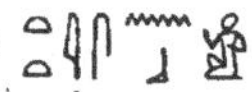

Text: [hieroglyphs].

F. right side. A similar group to *E*, with the following texts above the two seated persons:—

[hieroglyphs]

The inscription above the man making offerings has been covered by white-wash, and it is only possible to read the following signs:—

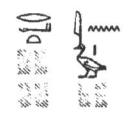

[hieroglyphs]

CHAPTER III

THE FUNERARY STATUETTES FROM TOMB OF TETA-KY

By Percy E. Newberry

THE discovery of Model Sarcophagi containing Funerary Statuettes in small holes on the four sides of the entrance to the mummy shaft (see Pl. II and p. 18) of Teta-ky's tomb is of considerable interest; it is, I believe, the first recorded instance of shawabti figures having been found in such positions. They were placed in the four holes in pairs; each model coffin and figure bears a different name, but curiously enough, that of Teta-ky, whose body was buried in the sarcophagus chamber at the bottom of the shaft, does not occur. Each model coffin consists of a rectangular box and lid of wood; the lid, having uprights at each end, is curved in section ⌒ : outside, the lid and box is painted white, with three blue vertical bands on box, and the lids are inscribed in black ink with the name of the person for whom the shawabti figure in the sarcophagus was made (Pl. X. 1). Each shawabti figure is of wood carved to represent a human mummy with arms crossed over chest, face and hands gilt, head-dress blue, and body white (Pl. X. 2). Each figure is also inscribed with the usual shawabti text in horizontal lines across the front and sides of the body. The people for whom these figures were carved are: (1) the 𓄿𓏤𓉐𓅓𓈖𓏌𓂋𓏤𓊵𓏏𓊪 'Overseer of the Garden of Amen, Ra-hotep'; (2) 𓋴𓈖𓃀 (vars. 𓋴𓈖𓃀 and 𓋴𓈖𓃀) 'Sen-senb'; (3) 𓏏𓊪𓄤 'Teta-nefer'; (4) 𓏏𓂝𓈖 'Teta-an'; (5) 𓏏𓂝𓂋𓂝 'Teta-em-ra'; (6) 𓇋𓅓𓂝 'Ÿma'; (7) 𓂋𓋴 'Res'; and (8) 𓋴𓈖𓃀𓅱 'Senbu'. The first two names, it should be observed, are those of Teta-ky's father and mother; probably the remaining six are also of other members of his family. We may, therefore, hazard the conjecture that these eight shawabti figures were placed at the opening of the shaft in the belief that they would protect, or 'answer for', their relation Teta-ky, whose body was interred below.

Besides the Funerary Statuettes described above, a large number of figures in Model Sarcophagi[1] were discovered in the four niches in the wall on the west

---

[1] On the early history of these Model Sarcophagi and Statuettes see Spiegelberg and Newberry's *Theban Necropolis*, pp. 26–9.

THE FUNERARY STATUETTES

side of the main court (Pls. I, II, p. 13). These Model Sarcophagi are of painted pottery, mud, or wood, the boxes are rectangular or oval in shape, with lids having uprights at each end; some of them bear inscriptions (Pl. XI). The figures are all of wood roughly carved to represent human mummies, and some of them are inscribed (Pl. XII. 2). The inscriptions, written in linear hieroglyphs or in hieratic, are of five types:—

(1) Giving only the name of the person for whom they were made.

(2) The simple *de hetep seten* formula to Osiris: e.g.

(3) The *de hetep seten* formula to Osiris, Lord of Busiris and Abydos.

(4) The *de hetep seten* formula to Osiris with name of dedicator added; e.g. '(dedicated) by his son who makes to live his name Teta-an.'

(5) The shawabti text in its early form: 'Oh! this shawabti, if Teta-ky in the underworld is summoned to do work for a man according to his duties, to cultivate the fields, to flood the banks (for irrigation purposes), or to carry sand from west to east. Behold I am there to do it.'

The personal names occurring on these shawabti figures are typical of the period immediately preceding the XVIIIth Dynasty. I arrange them in alphabetical order.

Aahmes.

Aahmes-sa-pa-ar.

Aah-hetep.

Antef.

Atef.

Ŷma.

Pa-khnems.

Nekhtu.

Ra-hotep.

Res.

Sena.

Sen-senb.

Senbu.

Tahuti.

FROM TOMB OF TETA-KY

Tahutý-aah.

Tahutimes.

Teta.

Teta-an.

Teta-ankh.

Teta-em-ra.

Teta-mesu.

Teta-nefer.

Teta-hemt.

Teta-sa.

Teta-senb.

Teta-ky.

Table for offerings (Pl. XII. 1) with rectangular depressions pierced with holes for draining to spout, and inscribed with the *de hetep seten* formula to Osiris Khent-amenti, and to Osiris, Lord of Busiris and of Abydos, that he may give offerings for the *Ka* of the Royal Son, Teta-ky. The horizontal line across the lower part of the table for offerings gives:—

(1) The name and titles of Teta-ky's father and (2) of his mother, the .

A fragment of a statue of Teta-ky bears the following legend:—

'Mayor in the Southern City (i.e. Thebes) Teta-ky, justified'. This is the earliest known reference to the office of a Mayor of Thebes.

CHAPTER IV

EXCAVATIONS IN THE VALLEY OF DÊR EL BAHARI

By Howard Carter

The panoramic view given in Pl. XIII clearly shows the nineteen different sites that were excavated and examined in this particular part of the necropolis during 1909 and 1910. Many were experimental excavations made on the chance of there being hidden tombs, but as several sites gave no results it is unnecessary to describe them.

Site 3. A tier of tombs, plundered, and most of them used in later times, probably by Copts, as dwellings.

In the corner of the court of the principal tomb of this series, under a fallen stone divisional wall (original), was a number of long and well-made pottery cones, uninscribed; the position and state in which they were found, the wall having fallen and covered them at an early period, gives us reason to suppose that they belong to the tomb and are of the XIth Dynasty (see Fig. 6, p. 8). Besides these cones, a very rough sandstone table of offerings without inscription, two Coptic pots, one with a wooden lid, some fragments of leather sandals, and a granite colour-grinder, were found dispersed in the drifted sand.

Site 4. A large tomb, facing west, high up on the mountain slope, with a causeway some twenty-five metres broad, walled on either side with rough stones, and leading down the face of the hill.

Like the tomb itself the façade is hewn in the rock; its right and left wings and overhead retaining wall, now mostly destroyed, were built of mud-brick.

The passage and chambers being open for many centuries the task here was to clear the façade court, into which its walls had fallen and been covered with rubbish drifted in from the desert above. It was discovered that the floor of the court, owing to the sloping rock bed, had been levelled and made good with stone rubble faced with lime mortar. The enormous fissures in the rock which ran through from side to side along its transverse axis had been treated in the same way. In the centre of the court, before the tomb entrance, was a large square shaft, sunk into the rock and formed mostly out of the natural fissures, previously mentioned, which had been utilized by the ancients in its construction. At the bottom of this shaft was the sarcophagus chamber, with its doorway blocked by a sandstone portcullis of one piece, measuring two metres high and one and a half metres broad. The sarcophagus chamber was rectangular in shape, low, and just large enough to receive the burial, i.e. the sarcophagus with the funereal equipment. At the south-east side of the court, buried beneath the fallen bricks of that side wing, is a small unfinished chamber.

The total area of the court had some two metres of earth covering it, and in the upper surface there were many cylindrical beads, a blue paste scarab (uninscribed), and two rough limestone heart-scarabs covered with blue paint. On the floor-level were fragments of funeral boat figures in wood, and a torso in limestone of one of the original occupants of the tomb (Pl. XVIII. 1 and 2). Covered by comparatively recent workings were two iron spear-heads.

In the shaft, which was filled with earth, were more cylindrical beads, some gilt, a black amber head, an obsidian eye-pupil from a coffin, a fragment of a crystal bead, the head and fractured pedestal of the limestone torso found in the court (Pl. XVIII. 1 and 2); also many burnt pieces of wood from coffins and figures including a rough table of offerings in limestone. The fractured pedestal had upon it the following partially erased inscription :—

The sarcophagus chamber was plundered and three parts full of rubbish. Access to it was obtained in ancient times by means of an opening forced between the top of the portcullis and lintel of the doorway. Its contents were smashed and burnt. Beads and small fragments of the objects of the burial were all that remained.

The side chamber of the court, mentioned above, was completely choked with drifted sand and had no antiquities in it at all.

Though among the objects found there were many of the XXIInd Dynasty, or even of a later period, the larger portion were certainly of the original XIth Dynasty burial; which, judging from the scanty remains, must have been very fine in quality, and of some high state official, but there was no inscription to tell us who he was.

Site 5. A depression in the surface of the hill slope, which proved to be a rock-cut court with sepulchral chambers on both sides and at its northern end (Pl. XV).

Almost at the commencement of its excavation the men came across the small chamber on the east side, containing the coffin of an adult burial untouched since the time it was deposited there. The entrance to this chamber was walled in with stones mixed with bricks and pieces of pottery, and it was found intact with the exception of a small opening at the top accidentally made by the workmen before discovering its real nature.

Later on, at the opposite side of the court, another small chamber was disclosed, but it proved to be unfinished.

Lastly, at the end of the court, a large chamber containing burials of seven adults and one child was found to be untouched. The sealing of the entrance was in perfect condition and was constructed like the other with similar stones and bricks (Pl. XIV. 1 and 2). The chamber was about two-thirds full of rubble, upon which the coffins were deposited, the first two having a slight excavation made for them. The first two coffins were placed side by side with their heads towards the east; they were covered by a pink shawl and chain garlands of leaves; with, beside the first one, a bouquet of cornflowers. This was evidently the last tribute paid to the dead placed in this sepulchre (see Pl. XVII. 3). The rest of the coffins, seven in all, belonging to a previous interment, and of a different type, were lying north and south with their heads to south. They were crowded together as if to make room for the latter burials. Some of these latter coffins had pieces of mummy-cloth upon them; the last of all some fragments of a decayed garland.

The east side-chamber was quite clean, and the coffin in it was placed exactly east and west with its head to the west.

After the removal of the coffins the large chamber was carefully explored. At the far end the commencement of an uncompleted pit was found, and at the entrance the remains of the early brick wall that originally closed the doorway were uncovered.

From the style of this tomb, the brickwork that closed the doorway, together with the pottery and some cones found in the rubbish, it clearly belongs to the earlier epoch of this district, the roughness of form being mostly owing to the inferior rock in which it is hewn (a conglomerate of lime and flints striated with *Tafle*). The beginning of a chamber on the west side of the court had been abandoned on account of some large flint-boulders embedded in the conglomerate which had prevented further progress, and the chamber on the east side was made in its stead. Neither of these cuttings seem to belong to the original design; they were most probably made by the usurpers found within the tomb: the fact that the floor-level of the completed side-chamber was the same as that of the rubbish drifted into the courtyard and tomb before its usurpation, I think, corroborates the above conjecture.

The burials in detail are as follows:—

1. *A*. (Pl. XVI. 3). A coffin containing inner case and mummy of a man named [hieroglyphs] Pa-de-Amen, [hieroglyphs] son of Pa-de-khonsu by the lady [hieroglyphs] Maartu.

Outer Case. Of wood, top of lid flat, with the face, head-dress, ornamental collar, and vertical line of hieroglyphs down the centre, painted.

Inner Case. Of thin wood, very roughly made, and painted white, with the four 'Amenti' figures painted in colour upon the chest. The vertical inscription on the front gives the *de hetep seten* formula to Osiris, and the name [hieroglyphs]

Reth-ar-es, which seems to have no connexion with the other names mentioned on the outer case.

The mummy was swathed in (1) the outer covering, consisting of a pink shawl bound by three longitudinal and seven transverse yellow bandages, (2) the inner covering of numerous narrow swathing bands bound round the body as well as crossways, with folded pieces of linen napkins and pieces of shawls stuffed in the hollow parts. Among these numerous wrappings were pieces embroidered with small blue patches woven into the fabric, some had their edges fringed, and many were much worn and darned.

The body was of a male adult, middle aged, with the hands placed at the sides.

1. *B.* A coffin containing a mummy of a lady named [hieroglyphs], Maartu (Pl. XVI, Fig. 1).

The coffin is far more elaborate than the former one, and generally finer both in workmanship and painting. The scenes painted upon it are of the deceased witnessing the weighing of her heart against the feather of truth in the presence of two apes representing *Thoth*, the devouring monster *Lord of Duat*, the goddess of truth *Maat*, *Horus*, *Osiris*, *Nephthys*, and two children of *Horus*. Below, the spirits of *Ash-Mut* and winged figures of *Ra* on either side.

Round the case, on the two outer sides and end, is a band of coloured hieroglyphs; and in the interior on the bottom, a painted figure of the goddess *Mut* surmounted by the winged *Horus*.

All the inscriptions give the *de hetep seten* formula invoking the gods in favour of the deceased, they also give her name and parentage [hieroglyphs], Maartu justified before Osiris. [hieroglyphs], Daughter of Amenhetep-en-auf. [hieroglyphs], Her Mother, the Lady of the House Nanu-nes-her.

The mummy was enveloped in a well-preserved dark terra-cotta coloured linen shroud, tied underneath and held in position by several narrow bands of brown and yellow linen, making a rich piece of colour and delicious harmony in contrast to the clean white and decorated interior of the coffin. Lying at the head was a fillet of leaves, like a diadem, sewn together and adorned with tiny petals of flowers (Pl. XVII. 2). The swathings under the shroud were similar to the first mummy (1. *A*), with the exception that the linen was coarser and the bandages broader (185 mms.). Among the folds were four *Amenti* figures and one *Bennu* bird in wax (Pl. XVII. 2); these were placed on the right vertical nipple line and on a level with the base of the Xephisternum.

The body was of a female adult of approximately thirty-five years of age The hands were placed between the thighs.

2. *B.* Coffin containing a mummy of a man named [hieroglyphs] Pa-de-Khonsu.

The decoration of the coffin and the manner of mummification of the body were both similar to 1. *A*. Some of the linen bandages had markings in light and dark blue, and red striated with dark blue running the whole length, woven into the stuff; and, like the others, many of the bandages were mended.[1]

The genealogy of these three persons was as follows:—

    Amenhetep-en-auf = Nanu-nes-her (of coffin 2. *B*)
    Pa-de-Khonsu = Maartu (of coffin 1. *B*)
    Pa-de-Amen (of coffin 1. *A*).

The meaning of the bandages being in so many cases carefully darned and mended might be explained by the inscriptions found on the walls of the tombs of the New Kingdom—a part of the ritual and last words of the relatives before the mummy when depositing it for ever in the tomb. 'Woe, woe, ... Alas this loss! the good shepherd has gone to the land of Eternity; he who willingly opened his feet to going is now enclosed, bound, and confined. He who had so much fine linen, and so gladly put it on, *sleeps now in the cast-off garments of yesterday.*'[2] The mummy bandages are strips torn nearly in every case from larger pieces like shawls and garments.

The second group of coffins, 3. *B* to 7. *B* (see Pl. XV), are of slightly smaller dimensions, painted black, and of a much rougher type. Only one of them had traces of design upon it, and that was in yellow upon the black background. The mummies they contained, though in good preservation and simulating the others in fashion, did not in general display the same care as in the former series. The linen in which they were wrapped had similar markings and mends, but they were of a coarser nature, and in some cases the materials were quite worn and old rags.

Coffin 3. *B* bore the *de hetep seten* formula, but the name of the deceased was omitted.

The mummy in coffin 7. *B*, of a man not more than thirty years of age, had on the left arm, tied at the elbow, a very fine blue glazed steatite scarab (Pl. XVII. 1, also Fig. 9, p. 27).

The small child's coffin, 8. *B*, was of plain wood exceedingly roughly made, and it contained the remains of a young boy prepared in the same manner as the others.

This last group may possibly have relationship in common with the others, even though their class does not appear to be of so high a standing; but unfortunately we have no inscription or real indication to tell us; the existing evidences show two distinct families but tend towards their being within a short period of one another—perhaps not more than a century.

Site 6 had openings to tombs, but proved unproductive.

Site 7, in the open courtyard of a large tomb of the XIth Dynasty; many decayed funeral boats and granary figures, as well as pottery cones and potsherds, cast out in past times, were the only reward for its excavation.

---

[1] The Rev. Dr. Collin Campbell, who was with me at the time we discovered these coffins, kindly translated the formulae upon them.
[2] Erman, *A Handbook of Egyptian Religion*, p. 137.

EXCAVATIONS IN THE VALLEY OF DÊR EL BAHARI 27

Site 8. Here were tombs with mud-brick buildings in front of them, like dwellings of embalmers. Beads and amulets, and a broken *Tazza*[1] (table) in pottery, all of different periods, were here unearthed.

Site 10. A tomb with large open courtyard facing south. This was completely excavated. On the east side of the main door was a low single brick wall; between it and the east corner a shallow round hole in the floor, like that for a foundation deposit (see tomb No. 16). In the east wall of the court was a small chamber, its entrance passage was three parts full of sand, while the chamber itself was comparatively clean. It must have been open anciently for many years as the ceiling, walls, and even the pots in it, were covered with mason-bees' nests. Mingled with the rubbish were pots of peg-top shape (Pl. XVIII. 10), broken pieces of coffins, funereal cones (see Fig. 6), and human bones, all of different dates and occurring here accidentally. The pieces of coffin were eaten by white ants, a pest certainly foreign to this part of the Theban necropolis, and for that reason I believe these wooden fragments came from some other portion of the

Fig. 9. Scarab from Tomb No. 5.

Theban necropolis. There is reason to suppose that the courtyard was never finished; there were many huge stones protruding out of the rock and jutting into the yard. In this yard more pottery was found, with among them two small pieces of linen tied up and containing pellets, like masticated corn mixed with grains of wheat.

Sites 11 and 12 produced nothing of further interest than a palm-tree in front of one of the tombs (12) which had been planted there in Nile mud brought up from the cultivation.

Site 13, a large rubbish heap formed of the débris thrown out by the ancient workmen when making the neighbouring tombs.

Here our hopes were to find a grave covered and protected by stuff thrown over it. Such indeed was the case, for within a few days the greater part of the mound was cleared away and the mouth of a cutting exposed. Naturally this raised great expectations, as the chances were that it would be undisturbed. But, as nearly always happens to the excavator in such cases, it is the unsuspected that occurs; the tomb had never been completed!

Sites 15 and 16 were on the open desert close to one another. 15 proved

[1] Cf. similar tazza Pl. XVIII. 12.

to be unfruitful. 16, though it at first appeared to be more promising by there being plenty of artificial chippings, had but little interest outside the fact that it led to a cutting of an already pilfered tomb. At the entrance of this cutting, in a small hollow in the *Tafle* rock, on the west side, was a 'pocket' of barley, which was at first a puzzle, as it did not seem accidental. Afterwards, on thinking that it might be of the nature of a foundation deposit to the tomb, the opposite side was carefully searched, and a corresponding 'pocket' with barley was eventually found; thus proving the conjecture to be correct, and showing that the tombs here, like the royal ones in the Valley of the Kings,[1] had foundation deposits as was customary also in the temples.

At the doorway of this tomb a pottery pan offering like a 'Soul House' was found (Pl. XVIII. 16).

Site 17. Here a pair of rush sandals and a pottery female figure were the prizes of the last day's work of the season of 1909 among the sepulchres of this region.

In Pl. XVIII. 3 are shown examples of each type and shape of the XIth Dynasty pottery found in the above excavations. There were only two other examples of a later date (Coptic), and they were of the most common form; the numbers on the illustration refer to the sites they came from.

Continuing the work in the year 1910, the large mounds immediately east of the footpath leading to the Biban el Mulûk were thoroughly investigated. These extend north and south on the hill slope below the great rock-cut tombs which are situated under the cliff at the top. This work was divided into two sites, Nos. 18 and 19 (Pl. XIII) and placed under two reises. It produced practically nothing, being only an immense covering of stone chippings upon the *gebel* thrown out from the tombs above. Among this accumulation, which varied in depth from one to five metres, many horns of animals suggesting sacrifices, leather thongs from implements, broken timber, and *balanites* kernels (Pl. LXXIX) were found; in fact the refuse from the workmen who had been employed upon the sepulchral caverns above. Thus, in the two seasons, this half of the north side of the valley between the eastern foot hills at its mouth and the mountain path may be said to have been thoroughly explored, leaving but small chances of undiscovered tombs.

The men were then removed further westward, close to Hatshepsût's Temple, where parallel trenches, twenty-five to forty metres broad, were dug. They began at the base of the slope and were carried up, in some cases, nearly to the foot of the vertical cliff; the excavations were continued until the rock surface had all been exposed.

Trench 20, begun from the temple temenos, yielded the following results :—

1. On the flat of the valley bed, between the temenos and the rising ground, was disclosed the mutilated foundation of a large wall (Pl. XIX. 1), extending

[1] Carter, *Tomb of Hâtshopsitû*, Chap. VI, and Carter and Newberry, *Tomb of Thoutmosis*, pp. 1–5, Nos. 46001–46035.

EXCAVATIONS IN THE VALLEY OF DÊR EL BAHARI 29

east and west, two metres wide, and built of crude bricks stamped with the cartouches of Amenhetep I and Aahmes-nefert-ari (Pl. XXIII. 20).

2. Over and along the side of the wall were many irregularly built mud dwellings for workmen, made of stray bricks of the XIth and early XVIIIth Dynasties; they no doubt were the rest-houses of the builders of the Queen Hatshepsût's temple.

3. Among the huts, in a depression roughly enclosed by limestone blocks, were the roots and stem of a date palm, set in black soil. Below the roots of the tree were several pots and a broken limestone statuette, placed as offerings for the welfare of the palm (Pl. XIX. 2). The pots contained a mud sediment. The statuette, which seems to have been used also as an offering, has the following inscriptions upon it :—

Down front of dress

On front end of throne

On right side of throne (1)

(2)

(3)

(4)

(5)

On left side of throne (1)

(2)

(3)

(4)

(5)

On back of throne

They mention the 'True Royal Scribe, Scribe of the Altar of the Lord of the Two Lands', Amenemhat, called *Keriba* (the Son of) 'Scribe of the Altar' Amenhetep. It was dedicated by Amenemhat's brother, 'Who made to live his name,' 'The Royal Scribe,' Userhat.

4. A few metres above, in the first part of the hill slope, hewn in the *Tafle*, was a chamber (No. 21). The interior had been plastered and it appears to have been a kind of office for the clerk of the works for the Queen's temple. It contained a broken rush and wicker-work stool, fragments of a mat, a basket,

torn fragments of papyrus, clay pellets for seal impressions, and a donkey halter. Leading up to the entrance was a small causeway. The fragments of papyrus, forty-three in number, when fitted together, proved to be part of Chapter XLI of the 'Book of the Dead', a list of different names of Osiris.

5. Higher up, on the top of the low foot-hill, was a series of cells built against the second incline. In one of these was a washing slab made of sandstone, with a hole in the corner of its sunken bed to allow the water to drain into a cesspool below; this was perhaps the bathing-place for the workmen (Pl. XX. 2).

6. On the second incline, eight metres above the bath, was part of a 'serpentine' wall (Pl. XX. 1), a peculiar structure not uncommon in building operations. Such a wall was found near the unfinished part of the north colonnade of the Queen's temple. Another example was found this season in Site 14. Its specific purpose is not thoroughly understood, perhaps it was an economical method of making enclosures for the working staff. In this particular case the bricks used for it belong to different periods—the XIth Dynasty brick (black mud without straw) and stamped bricks of Amenhetep I, Aahmes-nefert-ari, and Hatshepsût; the latter shows that it cannot have been earlier than the date of the Thothmes family.

7. A natural fissure in the hill near by had been, in late times, converted into a group of small tomb-chambers (No. 22). They had in them the plundered remains of burials like those of site No. 5, found in the season's work of 1909 (p. 23).

Trench 23, the next trench (parallel and east of 20), produced little or nothing. More stamped bricks of Aahmes-nefert-ari and Amenhetep I were found, and the beginning of an unfinished tomb-shaft in which was a boulder bearing the name, written in black ink. , Mentu-hetep.

Full attention being required by the Birâbi excavations, the third parallel trench was not begun until after an interval of ten days, when the good services of Mr. Cyril Jones were obtained for this express purpose. Mr. Jones, with thirty men and sixty boys, steadily continued the work as before, the base of his trench (No. 26) reaching as far as the north-east corner of the temple inclosure wall. The part ascending the valley side was barren and only exposed a plundered XIth Dynasty tomb (No. 80), re-used as an habitation, and afterwards as the place of a later burial consisting of a wooden *dug-out* coffin. But, on turning round the corner of the temple enclosure, he discovered a most interesting historical cache, a foundation deposit of the Dêr el Bahari dromos (for the exact position of this deposit see Pl. XXIV). For this deposit a circular hole, three metres deep and 140 cms. in diameter, had been made, and lined with a mud-brick wall with rounded and plastered coping (Pl. XXI. 2). The interior was filled with greyish (local) sand sprinkled with grains of corn. But for some reason the whole of the deposit was not placed in it. The tools and implements were found in a smaller hole, simply dug in the ground a few feet away, and like the former pit it was filled with sand and grain.

In the main pit the objects, placed in groups under alternate layers of sand, were discovered in the following order :—A few inches below the surface, the skull of an ox (Pl. XXI. 1), and underneath it a group of pottery, whole and broken, one pot containing grain, another containing fruit of the *Nebbek* tree. Then came the jaw-bone and fore-leg of an ox (Pl. XXI. 1), a piece of bread, a square sample of wood, an ebony symbolical knot (Pl. XXII. 2. E), and an alabaster pebble (Pl. XXII. 2. N) elaborately inscribed. In the third batch another symbolical knot, of cedar wood, two samples of fine linen, broken pottery that had contained oil, wines and food-stuffs, and two samples of coarse linen. Lastly, a rush mat, a pitcher-carrier, a second rush mat, and under it a second pitcher-carrier, masses of broken pottery, including a vessel containing a sample of mortar. Below these was plain sand reaching to the bottom of the pit.

Those of the second hole, mostly implements, were placed apparently not in any particular order, and are given in the following list, and illustrated in Plate XXII. 2 :—A bronze axe (A), graver (B), and chisel (C) ; an adze with a bronze blade bound by leather thongs to its wooden handle (F) ; a wooden mallet (D), hoe (G), brick mould (H), and peg (J) ; two sieves, one of palm-leaf with coarse mesh (K), the other of *halfa*-grass, with fine mesh, and made of horse or donkey hair (L) ; a rushwork jar rest (?) (M) ; a smelting crucible made of sun-dried mud (I), and lastly a pottery dish and jar. Many of these models were quite large, about three-quarter actual size, and all in a most perfect state of preservation.

The two knots (Pl. XXII. 2. E) have engraved upon them [hieroglyphs], the 'Nebti' name and prenomen of Hatshepsût.

The alabaster pebble (Pl. XXII. 2. N) has also the following legend :—
[hieroglyphs]. It mentions that Queen Maat-ka-ra (Hatshepsût) made this monument for her father Amen-Râ, when she measured out for Amen the Dêr el Bahari temple. Among the broken débris of pottery found in the main cache were two fragments bearing the words [hieroglyphs] 'wine', and [hieroglyphs] 'roast meat'.

Types of the pottery are given in Plate XXII. 1. These vessels of red pottery have nearly all been dipped into colour of a terra-cotta hue. The lip, rim, and neck of the jars (D, F, H), the upper half of the bowls (E, G, I), the interior and rims of dishes (A, B, C), are all coloured in that manner.

There is no doubt that the pots were intentionally smashed when deposited, and that the probable reason for this breaking was to disperse their contents during the ceremony over the sand. From this cause most of the pots and potsherds were found adhering to one another, due to the spilt unguents as well as to the blood from the flesh-offering having dried and caked them together. This may be a reason for the more perishable objects being placed in a separate cache. The bones, shown in Plate XXI. 1, are those of a young beast, the ossification being that of an immature animal. They measure :—

Skull. Length from top of occipital tuberosity to end of the pre-maxilla,

457 mms. (approximate); width of frontal bone between orbits, 150 mms.; length of jaw, from the mandibula condyle to end of the sub-maxillary bone, 380 mms.

Fore-leg. Length of scapula, along scapula axis, 317 mms.; length of humerus, from the head to the tip of outer condyle, 283 mms.; length of radius, from head to the lower end, 287 mms.; maximum length of the great metacarpal, 215 mms.

Other details of interest brought to light by these excavations in these trenches are recorded below:—

1. A potsherd with charcoal sketch of a Sinaitic ibex upon it.

2. A fine ostracon, bearing, in hieratic, a receipt dated in 'The 11th year (? Thothmes III), third month of Summer, 24th day', for various articles given by the 'Mayor' Aahmes.

3. Fragments of a shawabti figure, of white and violet glaze, bearing the name and title 'Royal Scribe of the Altar', Ky-nefer. Date XIXth Dynasty.

4. A group of broken shawabti figures, blue faience, of Zed-Khensu-auf-ankh. Date XXIInd Dynasty.

5. Three jar seals—(i) bearing on top two cartouches, with only the two signs visible; (ii) has the cartouche ; (iii) on the top surface is a cartouche-formed impression but illegible, and painted on the side is the commencement of the cartouche in yellow on a blue ground.

6. A child's toy—an interesting little pack-horse with removable packages, made of clay and housed in a pot. The packs are supported by four vine-leaf stalks which are stuck into the animal's sides (Pl. XXIII. 1).

7. From the rubbish of the court in front of Tomb 30 a small bundle of linen containing a steatite scarab, a strip of plaited rushwork, and some diamond-shaped pieces of leather with minute multicoloured bead-work sewn upon them.

8. In two places the trenches cut through temple refuse heaps, one high upon the north side of the monument, the other at the north-east corner of the temenos. These heaps are certainly of great interest, and should one day be carefully worked through, for in them there are numbers of broken votive offerings, brought by the populace to invoke the aid and assistance of the local divinity. They consist of bronze, earthenware, blue glaze, Hathor heads, cows, *menats*, model bunches of grapes, rings, balls, sistrums, sphinxes, scarabs, scarab-shaped and cowroid beads (one bearing the name of Aahmes I), amulets, such as ears, eyes, and *Ankhs*, dishes, bowls and vases, some of which are of very large dimensions.

A full series of pottery is given in Pl. XXIII. 2.

Types. B, C, D, E, G, K, L, M are of rough red pottery.

A, F, lightly burnt mud and lenticular in shape.

I, red pottery, coloured white, and ornamented with black and red.

J, red pottery, whitened.

N, red pottery with black and red rings (fragment).

Plate LXXIX. 1 gives two examples of fig-basket found in the refuse heaps mentioned above.

Towards the end of the exploration of 1911 an attempt was made to discover the corresponding dromos deposit to that revealed by the work of Mr. Cyril Jones in 1910. The exact measurements of the position of the former one were taken, and laid down on the opposite side of the dromos; the spot thus indicated was dug, and within a few hours the second cache was exposed. It resembled the former one in every way, the only variant being that the inscription upon the alabaster pebble in this case was slightly different. It reads:— , 'The Good Goddess Maat-ka-ra, living, beloved of Amen Ra, Lord of the thrones [of the two lands].'[1]

This completes our three consecutive seasons' researches on the north side of the Dêr el Bahari Valley, which is mainly occupied by the early tombs of the XIth Dynasty.

[1] The deposit of implements was missing in this case.

WORK DONE IN THE BIRABI

CHAPTER V

THE SEVENTEENTH DYNASTY TOMB No. 9

By Howard Carter

The site between the native house 'Beit el Meleitên' and the village mosque, about one hundred and fifty metres north-east of the mouth of the Dêr el Bahari valley, was examined in 1908, and as it resulted in the discovery of a XVIIth Dynasty tomb (No. 9), it was continued in the following year 1909. We began by exhaustively clearing tomb No. 9 that for the sake of protection during the interim had been re-covered with earth. In 1908 the front court, pit, and pit-chamber had been investigated: in 1909 our attention was thus confined to the inner chamber only, but everything of interest was discovered during the earlier work.

During the work of 1908 the courtyard was found to contain great masses of pottery and mutilated mummies, and it was among these, on a rock ledge, that the important historical tablet referring to the expulsion of the Hyksos by the General Kamosi (see further description by Griffith, p. 86), and the second broken tablet were recovered. In the first chamber were found parts of a wooden painted Canopic box, with three of its jars in pottery painted to imitate alabaster (Pl. XXV. 1 and 2), among other destroyed remains of a plundered burial. But in 1909, owing to the depth and sliding nature of the rubbish, a more extensive excavation had to be made to open the main chambers. Little more was found here than further examples of pots, a child's coffin too decayed for preservation, and a reed burial of a poorer and much later man (for example see Pl. XLII. 3). The tomb consisted of a court formed by low stone and mortar walls, with a cutting in the centre leading to the entrance: this entrance or doorway gave access to a passage, cut in the rock, some six metres in length, which led to a rectangular chamber that apparently formed one of the sepulchral repositories. Cut in the floor of this chamber, on the west side, was a shaft nearly three metres deep, giving ingress to two other chambers, one above the other.

THE SEVENTEENTH DYNASTY TOMB NO. 9

It hardly seems credible that such a mass of pottery as was found in the rubbish outside could have all come from so small a tomb, and one is inclined to think that the greater part must have come from some neighbouring and perhaps larger tomb.

Plate XXVI gives the different types of the pottery vessels found here. The earthenware is fine in quality, deep red, with smooth surface, and of a soft nature. Some are of a yellowish-grey material, and examples of these are given in Plate XXVI. 2 (the five pieces on the right hand of the lower row). In the top illustration are shown three very fine specimens of complete jars with lids in red pottery with black lines round the circumference of their bellies.

The name on the Canopic box is Kati-nekht,

CHAPTER VI

CARNARVON TABLETS I AND II

By F. Ll. Griffith

The writing tablet (Carnarvon Tablet I) is a document of the highest historical importance, preserving as it does a contemporary record of the conflict of the Theban Dynasty with the Hyksos. On the face of the tablet eight lines of hieratic contain the introduction to the famous Proverbs of Ptah-hetep, setting forth how the Wazir Ptah-hetep, son of a king, spoke to his King Assa of the advance of old age upon him and the diminution of all his powers, and requested that he might delegate his duties to his son, whom he would instruct in the words and ways of the Ancients. The King accorded his request and bade him proceed, and thus originated the rules of good conduct which go by the name of the old Wazir. The text[1] of the tablet shows some considerable differences of reading from the only other copy known—that in the Prisse Papyrus.

Below this fragment of philosophy are marked the lines of a draught-board, in squares 10 × 8. Four of the compartments contain hieratic signs indicating their place in the game.

The historical text on the other side consisted of no less than seventeen long lines. Unhappily the flaking of the stucco[2] about the fracture has robbed us of one line and of the greater part of two more. The text is singularly difficult, and this great gap, added to some minor imperfections, further obscures the meaning. In the following brief analysis I have had the help of a number of excellent readings suggested by Mr. A. H. Gardiner.

The text is dated in the seventh year of King Kamosi, who is described as beloved of Amen-Ra, the god of Karnak. His Majesty was speaking in his palace unto the court and nobles who attended him, 'Consider for what is my might! One prince is in Avaris, another in Ethiopia!' He continues to discourse of the division of the land and mentions Memphis and Cusae in an obscure context. 'And the nobles of his court said, "Behold, the Asiatics have approached (?) unto Cusae, they have drawn (?) their tongues in one manner, [saying?]

---

[1] Jequier, *Le Papyrus Prisse et ses variantes* (Pap. Brit. Mus. 10371 and 10435, Tablette Carnarvon au Caire), Paris, 1910; Maspero, *Recueil*, Vol. XXXI, p. 146.

[2] The tablet is made of wood covered with stucco of fine plaster for a writing surface.

We are happy with our Black Land as far as Cusae, ... our barley is in the papyrus-marshes . . . . . our barley is not taken."' The meaning of this is very uncertain. Then after a gap, 'they are painful to His Majesty,' perhaps referring to the replies of the countries.

After a long gap, '[The king, mighty in] Thebes, Kamosi, protector of Egypt [said?], "I have gone north victorious to drive back the Asiatics by the command of Ammon: the plans of my army have succeeded: every mighty man was before me like a flame of fire, the mercenaries of the Mezaiu (Nubians) were like the threshing instrument (?) to seek out the Satin and to destroy their places: the East and the West were successful (?), the army rejoicing at each thing in its order. I led the victorious mercenaries of the Mezaiu . . . . Teta the son of Pepa in Nefrus, I allowed him not to escape (?). I stopped the Asiatics, I freed (?) Egypt . . . . . . I was in my ship, my heart rejoicing! When day dawned, I was on him like a hawk: at a moment of . . . . . I drove him out, I hacked down his wall, I slew his people, I caused my soldiers to embark like wolves with their prey, with slaves, cattle . . . . honey, dividing their property; their hearts . . . . . ."' Another very obscure line follows. As Ahmosi, the successor of Kamosi, completed the overthrow of the Hyksos by the capture of Avaris early in his reign, one may conjecture that this text gives us the stage in the expulsion of the Hyksos when they were driven from Middle Egypt and confined to Lower Egypt by the Theban power. The latter had also to contend with a rival in Nubia, who was likewise crushed by Ahmosi.

It is remarkable that the titles of Kamosi as given here do not agree with those upon the Treasure of Ahhotp; the handwriting proves that Lord Carnarvon's tablet (Carnarvon Tablet I) had been written within a few years of the events recorded in it. The publication of the facsimile is certain to rouse the interest of every student of one of the most fascinating problems in oriental history.

The fragments of the second tablet (Carnarvon Tablet II), facsimiled in Plate XXIX, have not yet been translated.

CHAPTER VII

THE 'VALLEY'-TEMPLE OF QUEEN HATSHEPSÛT

By Howard Carter

ADJOINING the site of Tomb 9 is the 'Valley'-Temple to the Dromos of Hatshepsût's Mortuary Chapel at Dêr el Bahari (Site 14, Pl. XXX).

It was first discovered by the excavation of the tomb No. 9, which exposed some of its stone-work, and it was a surprise to find here, in such a well-known place, a finely built limestone construction of considerable proportions quite near to the surface.

At the beginning this building was a puzzle to us, the part revealed in season 1909 being only a long piece of the outside wall which gave but few data, and thus became a source of much speculation as to its meaning. This wall ran east and west, having a base measurement of 2·60 metres broad with its outer faces sloping— their 'batter' being 4 cms. in every rise of 25 cms. Its construction consists of two outer skins of small well-made limestone blocks built upon sandstone foundation slabs, with, in the middle, a core of stone and mortar rubble mixed with sand. In it was a doorway, about half-way along the length cleared, which opened out to the north—its door-jambs being on that side. The eastern extremity of the excavation then made, showed that in that direction it descended. Under the doorway a search was made for a deposit but with no result, though at the west end, the part of the wall first discovered, there was a pocket of sand which seemed to have belonged to something of that nature.

The extensive exploration of this site in 1910 clearly determined that it was an unfinished portion of a building of Terrace-Temple form; and that the wall, which had given rise to many theories, was only its northern boundary wall (Pl. XXXI. 1 and 2).

The intended scheme of this unfinished building seems to have been an Upper and a Lower Court, divided by a single Colonnaded Terrace (see plan and section, Pl. XXX), similar somewhat to Hatshepsût's Mortuary Chapel at Dêr el Bahari. It is, however, all in the very early stages of construction, the wall itself being the only part that shows any signs of completion. Very possibly, in earlier times, a great deal more of the structure existed, for it had been used as a quarry for limestone at some late period.

THE 'VALLEY'-TEMPLE OF QUEEN HATSHEPSÛT 39

In detail, the 'battered' boundary wall, averaging nearly 6 metres in height, was capped by a coping-stone curved on the top. The base of its outer face declines from the level of the Upper Court down to the level of the Lower Court, a matter of nearly 4·50 metres difference in level; while, on the inner side, the base is horizontal and takes the levels of the two courts. When looking at the plan (Pl. XXX) it will be noticed that the wall gradually swells on the outer face between the two sections, viz. the Upper and Lower Courts, and suddenly returns to its normal thickness. This can be explained by the fact that a 'battered' surface must necessarily spread as it descends to a lower level. It was at this point (the level of the Lower Court) blended back to the normal base measurement of the wall by a small angle of masonry (see Pl. XXXI. 1).

The Lower Court, as far as the excavation shows us, seems to be a plain open quadrangle, abutting a raised terrace colonnade, of which one base alone of the square columns of the Terrace still exists. Above this Terrace, the back of which

FIG. 10. HIERATIC INSCRIPTIONS FROM 'VALLEY'-TEMPLE.

served as a retaining wall, is what we can only suppose to be the Upper Court, and like the lower one is a square open enclosure. On the north side of this Upper Court is a doorway (mentioned above) in the boundary wall. Behind the masonry of the Terrace are the remains of the original mud-brick scaffold for supporting the earth of the Upper Court while building the back stone wall of the Terrace itself. The masonry in some cases is good, while in others it is of the roughest kind, and in many parts the surfaces have been left undressed.

Hieratic inscriptions, written in ink upon the under surfaces of the stone blocks from the walls (see Fig. 10), name the architect 'the Second Priest of Amen, Pu-am-ra', whose tomb (dated Thothmes III) is in the Assasif.

This fixed the date of the monument to the reign of Queen Hatshepsût or Thothmes III, but to which of these two reigns, and for what use the edifice was intended, still remained unanswered for want of further data.

Later, in the year 1911, we at last discovered a foundation deposit of the building (see Pl. XXX, marked Hatshepsût's Deposit A and B), and here a small

40 THE 'VALLEY'-TEMPLE OF QUEEN HATSHEPSÛT

brick pillar and model tools gave the owner's name, 'Maat-ka-ra' (the prenomen of Queen Hatshepsût), and on the tools themselves was the name of the building 'Zeser-zeseru'. The occurrence of these names shows at once that the building formed part and parcel of the Dêr el Bahari edifice, and from its position it is clear that the building was the termination of the dromos of the famous temple—in fact its Portal or 'Valley'-Temple—assimilating in idea the older plan of the pyramid chapels and 'valley'-temples connected by great causeways of the pyramids at Gizeh, the tomb which takes the place of the pyramid being in this case on the opposite side of the cliff in the valley of the Tombs of the Kings.

The foundation deposit, like that of the other end of the dromos found in 1910 (p. 31), was composed of two separate groups, (1) a pillar of ten mud-bricks, each stamped with the Queen's prenomen ⟨ ⟩ (see Plan, Pl. XXX, marked A); and (2) a few metres from it (see Plan, Pl. XXX, marked B) were found two model adzes in wood inscribed with the following hieroglyphic inscription:— ⟨ ⟩. These were fully four metres below the pavement level of the Upper Court of the 'Valley'-Temple.

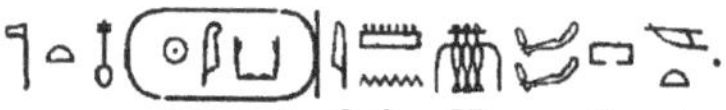

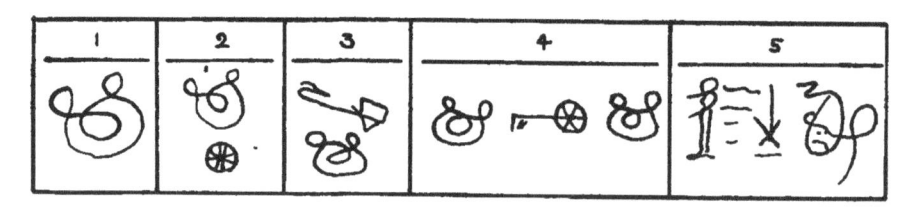

Fig. 11. Graffiti on Stones from 'Valley'-Temple.

Objects found during the excavation of, and belonging to this monument, were:—

1. Lying loosely in the rubbish, a very fine specimen of a workman's hoe (Pl. XXXII. 3).

2. In the masonry of the corner of the terrace colonnade, a mason's mallet, exactly similar to those found in the Queen's Temple of Dêr el Bahari by the Egypt Exploration Fund in 1893–1896.

3. Generally distributed about the site were stamped bricks of the Queen (Pl. XXXII. 2), and also two larger bricks stamped with the cartouches of Thothmes I and Maat-ka-ra in conjunction, with the epithets ⟨ ⟩ and ⟨ ⟩ under their names (Pl. XXXII. 4).

4. A red crystalline sandstone tally-stone bearing the prenomen of Hatshepsût (Pl. XXXII. 1).

THE 'VALLEY'-TEMPLE OF QUEEN HATSHEPSÛT

5. Low down, about the foundation level and half-way along the lower section of the north boundary wall, was a mass of stones with dressed faces for building. These stones, numbering seventy-six in all, were stacked with their faces downwards. Out of these stones thirty-five had painted in black upon their faces the signs ⌢, 'the Good Festival', with one of the batch having the supplementary word ⌢, 'Brick'. Another had an illegible inscription beginning with the sign ⌢ and the word 'Amen'. Six had peculiar signs or quarry marks scrawled in charcoal (see Fig. 11). That on the fifth stone can be read as ⌢ [○], the name of the Queen's architect Sen-mut. The sign ⌢, *Sent*, that occurs on four of the other stones might be interpreted as 'a ground plan'.

CHAPTER VIII

PTOLEMAIC VAULTED GRAVES

By Howard Carter

Covering the upper stratum of the sites explored in the Birâbi were numerous brick-vaulted graves, mostly found not more than a metre or so beneath the surface rubbish (Pl. XXXIII).

Probably when these vault-graves were first made they actually stood above the surface, their superstructures being in all probability intended to be exposed, as would be gathered from the fact of their external walls showing, in some cases, painted decoration upon the plaster still adhering to them (Pl. XXXIV. 2). In every case they were found to be plundered, and in the course of examining some forty examples that we came across, we rarely found but the very slightest traces of the burials they once contained. And all that we were able to gather from these vestiges of the actual interments was that they were of the Ptolemaic period, but almost pure Egyptian in type. This fact thoroughly corroborates Mr. Edgar's statement that 'during the Ptolemaic period many of the Greek inhabitants began to adopt the practice of mummification. At first naturally their custom went to the native undertakers, and their mummies were decorated just like those of the Egyptians. Here and there as time goes on, signs of Greek influence begin to appear. But it is not till the Roman period that the style becomes what could be properly called Greek.'[1]

In these graves the coffins were of rectangular and anthropoid form, and the mummies were enclosed in canvas cartonnages covered with stucco elaborately decorated with pictures of the numerous Egyptian deities and ritual inscriptions of the usual formulae. Their funerary objects were glazed faience bowls of several colours, such as many different blues, violets, &c.; small roughly glazed shawabti figures; porcelain deities and amulets; painted carved wood *Ba*-birds; erotic figures in faience; and beads, &c. There were also vases and bowls in

---

[1] Edgar, *Cat. Gen. C. M. Graeco-Egyptian Coffins*, pp. ii, iii.

pottery; and in two instances we found a bowl of copper gilt (Fig. 12) and vases in lead, left or forgotten by the plunderers.

Luckily the substructure of these graves was nearly always found intact, and likewise in many cases their superstructure. And by this we were able to gather that it was a common custom for them to have small brick vestibules or shrines before their entrances; and that under the floors of either the outbuildings or the vaulted chambers themselves, one or more amphorae were buried for water or food for the dead (Pl. XXXIV, Fig. 1); the mouths of these jars were covered by inverted bowls and sealed with mud.

In one of these sealed vessels, found under the floors, two demotic papyri were discovered (see description by Spiegelberg, p. 46); in others were date cakes,

FIG. 12. GILT COPPER VESSEL FROM PTOLEMAIC VAULTED GRAVES.

grain, and seeds of different kinds; and in the corner of one of the small outer chambers a batch of forty-seven Ptolemaic coins (p. 44). The fortunate discovery of the papyri and coins, treated hereafter, give data for fixing the period of these vaults to the earlier Ptolemaic times.

With regard to construction, these vault-graves built of mud-brick are of a rectangular longitudinal shape. The side walls, one and a half bricks thick, are from six to ten bricks high, while the end walls are carried up to the height of the crown of the vault. On the inner face of the side walls a ledge is left, half-way up, for a support to carry the vaulted roof (the outer faces are run up as high again to receive the thrust of the vault). The vaulted roof, one brick in thickness, has its rings leaning against the end wall, starting at the foot with first one brick on either side, then two, three, and so on, until the feet of these incomplete rings are far enough out to allow a complete leaning ring to be formed with its crown actually touching the end wall at the top. To this complete ring the bricks of the subsequent rings of the vault are stuck, thus avoiding the force of gravity and enabling the vaulting to be built without the aid of timber centring. This is a method by which a barrel-vault can be made, technically known as a *flown-vault*, and which is known and used by natives in Egypt at the present day.

For strength and to reduce the thrust, the vault is of parabolic section and not truly semicircular.

Access to these vaulted chambers was sometimes by means of an arched opening in the end wall covered by the vestibule (Pl. XXXIV. 2), or, when the

FIG. 13. PTOLEMAIC COINS FROM VAULTED GRAVES.

latter structure was wanting, by a chimney-like hole at the top of one end of the barrel-vault.

The flat vault bricks (34 × 16 × 6 cms.) have grooves on one side to allow the mortar to have a better and firmer grip—a very necessary point for this style of vaulting.

The group of forty-seven Ptolemaic copper coins (Fig. 13), the preservation of which is unusually good for coins found in Upper Egypt, new coinage rarely getting so far south, belong apparently to the dominations of Ptolemies III and IV. They are of four sizes and in detail are as follows:—

	Av. weight grammes.	Av. diam. mms.

10. *Obv.* Head of Zeus Amon to right.
    Rev. Eagle on thunderbolt to left; cornucopia in field in front of eagle.
    Mints: ♣. ΔΙ. Ε.   73·0   42·0

PTOLEMAIC VAULTED GRAVES

		Av. weight *grammes.*	Av. diam. *mms.*
6.	*Obv.* Head of Zeus Amon to right. *Rev.* Eagle on thunderbolt to left; cornucopia in field in front of eagle. Mints: ΔΙ. ΣΕ. Σ. ₤.	67·0	40·5
17.	*Obv.* Head of Zeus Amon to right. *Rev.* Eagle on thunderbolt to left, head turned to right; cornucopia in field over back of eagle. Mints: Ε. ₤. Ρ. Λ.	48·0	39·0
14.	*Obv.* Head of Zeus Amon to right. *Rev.* Eagle on thunderbolt to left; cornucopia in field in front of eagle. Mints: ₤. ΔΙ. Σ.	35·5	34·0

CHAPTER IX

DEMOTIC PAPYRI AND OSTRACA

By Wilhelm Spiegelberg

The two papyri which I propose to call in future Papyrus Carnarvon I and II are of great importance on account of their date.[1] They both bear the protocol of a local king who reigned in Upper Egypt under Ptolemaios Epiphanes (205–181 B.C.). The king is named Harmachis, and so far there are known to exist only three other contracts of his time, two in the Berlin Museum (Demotic Pap. Berlin, Nos. 3142-4, 3145), dated in his third and sixth years, and another mentioned in the *Revue Égyptologique*, I, p. 121 (the collection in which it is preserved not being mentioned), is dated in his fifth year.

The two Carnarvon papyri are dated in the fourth year, and their protocol reads: 'Year 4 in the month of Athyr of King Harmachis, living eternally, beloved of Isis, beloved of Amonrasonter, the great god.'

In the first papyrus (Pap. Carnarvon I, Pls. XXXV, XXXVI) a woman Senobastis sells 1½ cubits of waste land (about 40 square metres), situated in the endowed land of the god Amon near a place P-ohi-n-p-mehen, to a herdsman(?) and slave of the god Amon, Psenesis.

The second papyrus (Pap. Carnarvon II, Pls. XXXVIII, XXXIX) concerns a sale of arable land in the same region between the herdsman(?) and slave of the god Amon, Pachnumis and Paos bearing the same titles.

Paos and Psenesis were brothers, a fact which makes the two papyri part of the acts of the same family. They are signed by the same public notary, 'Petamenophis, the son of Petemestus, ... who writes in the name of the priests of the god Amonrasonter,' and among the sixteen witnesses on the verso of the papyri eleven are identical in both texts (Pl. XXXVII. 1 and 2).

These two documents concern two different sales of temple land in the same Theban region between different contractors, of whom two are members of the same family. As we know that in Ptolemaic and Roman times every sale was concluded by two documents, the agreement for sale ($συγγραφὴ$ $πράσεως$) and the contract of cession ($συγγραφὴ$ $ἀποστασίου$), it is evident that we have only

---

[1] I hope to publish a full translation of both texts with commentary shortly.

half of the complete acts of the two sales, viz. the sale agreements. Now in Pap. Carnarvon I on the right margin opposite line 4 there is a part of a sign (not given in the plate) which may be the end of a line of another text. This may belong to the lost contract of cession written upon the same roll as the existing written agreement. At any rate the two documents are not complete, they are only the sale agreements, and their juridical complements, i.e. the Cession Acts, may still turn up some day.

OSTRACA.

Among the thirty-three demotic ostraca, i.e. demotic inscriptions upon potsherds and limestone flakes, found among the Ptolemaic remains in the upper stratum of Site 14, and all of the Ptolemaic period, only one has a definite date.

It is of 'the year 21 of the kings Ptolemaios son of Ptolemaios and of Ptolemaios, his son,' i.e. of Ptolemaios II, Philadelphos, and his son Euergetes I (about 265-264 B.C.). The texts contain tax receipts, contracts, accounts, and lists of workmen.

One ostracon is of a quite unusual type (Pl. XXXVII. 3). Perhaps it is the receipt for the fee of a contract concerning a sale of land; the text is signed by Thothmosis, and has the date of 'the year 4 the 30th (?) Choiak'.

CHAPTER X

COLONNADE AND FOUNDATION DEPOSIT OF RAMESES IV

By Howard Carter

In 1911 many large paving slabs of limestone with positions of columns marked by circles chiselled upon them were uncovered (see plan, Pl. XXX. 40). These were immediately below a number of Ptolemaic vault-graves, and practically on the same level as the pavement of the Upper Court and some twenty-eight metres south of the boundary wall of the 'Valley'-Temple.

As far as the work of this season allowed, eleven of these substructures were revealed, giving enough proof that a late building of some kind, in part or complete, had existed there. The fact that lime-mortar still exists within the circles that marked the bases of the columns, proves that at least the lower part of the column drums once stood there. The builder of this double colonnade, running east and west, was proved to be Rameses IV by our finding under the north-east corner a deposit bearing his names. This deposit, placed in the sand and enclosed by a few bricks and not a metre and a half below the masonry, consisted of 148 electrum and faience objects excluding the barley grains, samples of red jasper, and matrices of emerald that were mixed with them.

Pl. XL illustrates a complete series of the different articles that formed the deposit:

Group 1. Plaques, made of electrum.
 „   2. Cartouches, of blue and violet glass.
 „   3. Plaques, of blue glazed faience.
 „   4. Cartouches, of blue glazed faience.
 „   5. Various objects, also of blue glazed faience.
 „   6. Samples of blue and violet glass rods, red jasper, and matrices of emerald.

The variants of the names of Rameses IV that occur among these objects are:

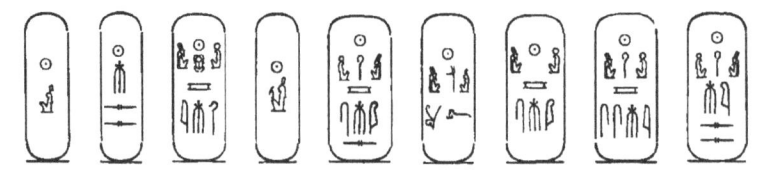

CHAPTER XI

OTHER ANTIQUITIES DISCOVERED

By Howard Carter

In the removal of the lower strata of Site 14 the mass of sand, amounting to many thousands of cubic metres, contained but few things to which any great importance could be attached. In fact, days were passed while extricating the masonry of the 'Valley'-Temple without hardly a single object coming to light. Among the few things discovered the most important were:—

1. A genealogical stela in limestone, measuring 44 × 29 cms., coloured, and of the 'Household of the mother of the *Mer Shen* of Amen, Zed-Amen-auf-ankh' (Pl. XLI). It mentions the following personages:—

The Lady Nes-ta-nebt-Asheru.
The Priest of Amen in Karnak, Hor.
His mother, the Lady Nes-ta-nebt-Asheru.
The Priest of Amen-Ra, Hor, son of the Priest Pedemut.
Her mother Ta-bak-en-ta-Ashat-qa.
The Governor of Thebes Hor-se-Ast, son of Zed-Aah.
The Chief Royal Scribe Bak-en-Khonsu, son of the Mayor of Thebes Auf-aa-hor.
His mother, the Lady Mes-per, daughter of the Priest of Amen-Ra Hor, son of Zed-Amen-uah-es.
The Chief Royal Scribe Hor, son of Zed-Amen-uah-es.
The mother of the Lady Nes-ta-nebt-Asheru, Nes-Khonsu-pa-khred.
The Priest of Amen-Ra Nekht-ef-mut.
Her mother, the Lady Ta-aa, daughter of the Priest of Amen Hor-kheb, son of Ahat.[1]

2. Along the sloping base of the boundary of the 'Valley'-Temple, on the north side, were three small mud-brick feretories or shrines. They were 'lancet-arch' in form, measuring 50 cms. high, 40 cms. broad, and rather more in length, with, in front, a small arched opening (Pl. XLII. 2). One was built against the wall, a little above the pavement level, and facing north; the others were some distance from the wall and facing east. In one were a few dried dates and leaves

---

[1] For this translation thanks are due to Professor Newberry.

(Pl. LXXIX), and near by at a lower level were the bones of a gazelle. These feretories may have been shrines erected to pet animals buried there, and possibly are of quite late date.

3. A stamped brick of Amenhetep II.

4. A stamped brick of Thothmes III.

5. Part of the back and leg of a bifold wooden chair, inlaid with ivory and ebony, and of an earlier date than the XVIIIth Dynasty (? XIIth Dynasty).

6. A wooden box, painted white, measuring 50 × 30 × 30 cms., which has on the under side of the lid four entries in hieratic (Pl. XLII. 4). They mention a date 'third month of winter season, day 10'; a 'Scribe of the Necropolis'; an 'Overseer of workmen', called Amen-renpet; an account of three vases of liquids; names of officials, and an account of grain, together with the name of a wood.[1]

7. Two burials of poor people. One was enveloped in rushes bound together with rope, the other with reeds (Pl. XLII. 3). The bodies in both cases had a single winding sheet, but show no signs of mummification. They appear to belong to a late epoch.

8. A wooden Osiride figure (Pl. XLII. 1) covered with bitumen and wrapped in linen. The arms, crossed over the breast, have in the right hand the *Flail*, and in the left hand the *Crook*, which are made of copper. Period XVIII (?) Dynasty. (It is similar to the bitumened figures found in the tombs in the Valley of the Kings.)

9. Shawabti figures of the Intermediate period in model coffins (Pl. XLIII). The most important specimens were:—

A. A wooden sarcophagus with figure wrapped in linen. The inscription in linear hieroglyphs gives the *de hetep seten* formula to Osiris, for offerings for *Nefer-ur*. The figure is dedicated by his 'sister' *Sedemt*.

B. A clay coffin with wooden shawabti, the lid crudely anthropoid in shape, and roughly decorated with green and yellow in the design of the *Rîshi* coffin type (see Pl. XLIII); the rough figure inside has green stripes painted upon it.

---

[1] The translation is due to Professor Newberry.

CHAPTER XII

THE LATE MIDDLE KINGDOM AND INTERMEDIATE PERIOD NECROPOLIS

By Howard Carter

DEEP below the foundations of the 'Valley'-Temple of Queen Hatshepsût in the Birâbi are rock-hewn tombs, or pit and corridor types, dating from the XIIth Dynasty on to the Intermediate Period.

This fact was first ascertained in 1910, and in that year twelve tombs of this necropolis were opened. Their exploration was continued in 1911, when four more were revealed, and three out of the four were thoroughly investigated.

All the graves examined during the two seasons had had their original burials previously pillaged: firstly, at a period not long after their origin, and certainly before the New Empire; and in certain instances a second time in the XVIIth or XVIIIth Dynasties, when some were re-used for odd burials.

These successive plunderings gave access to the white ants, the worst of all the enemies the explorer has to contend with. Often when a chamber is first entered its contents seem in comparatively good preservation, but on the slightest touch or movement they fall into a thousand fragments, their substance being riddled by these tiny insects.

The positions and plans of these tombs are shown in the Plan and Survey, Pl. XXX.

Corridor Tomb 24.

This was the first and most spacious among those opened in 1910. It had no less than eight chambers, a long passage, an open court, and a pit. It was only from the remains of funereal débris, discovered in the rubbish of an open depression in the rock (i.e. the court), that it was recognized that an early and violated tomb was in the course of being revealed. These fragments were:—

1. The cross-bars of an *Angarib* (bedstead made of plaited rope on a wooden frame supported by four legs).

2. The greater part of a wooden model boat of uncommon design.

52   THE LATE MIDDLE KINGDOM AND

3. A small piece of wood with beautiful cornelian inlay upon it from a coffin (?).

4. Broken pieces of cartonnage painted and gilded.

5. A part of the end of a square coffin, inscribed and giving the name [hieroglyphs] 'Ankhu'.

6. Another coffin board, inscribed with coloured hieroglyphs, reading— [hieroglyphs] giving the name 'Khety'.

7. A broken arrow-head of flint with serrated edges.

8. Pieces of leather sandals, pottery, and a portion of the neck of a jar with [hieroglyphs] Men-hetep written upon it.

9. A scribe's palette with two reed brushes (Pl. XLV. 3).

10. The hind half of an exquisitely made frog in glazed steatite, and the fore part of a lion in faience.[1]

When cleared enough to be entered the interior of the tomb presented a scene of utter despoliation. Its chambers were strewn with rubble mingled with bones, skulls, and tomb furniture, shattered and burnt, which only too well corroborated those traces of the ravages which had been found outside. In the central chamber was a burial—a wood dug-out coffin, anthropoid in form, the lid bound at head and shins with rope. Several days were spent in carefully searching the remains in this tomb, and by sifting the sand many times favourable results were obtained. These results are recorded below:—

Near the Entrance. A small wooden statuette and pedestal; upon the latter are three barely visible lines of hieroglyphs, in which the name [hieroglyphs] 'Ankhu' may possibly be traced, and if so it probably identifies the figure with the person mentioned on the coffin fragment found outside (Pl. XLIV. 1).

Doorway. A nude female figure in cedar wood, very much worn and originally coloured. She wears a heavy head-dress tied by a fillet on either side. Such figures were entered among the funerary complement for the personal use of the deceased (Pl. XLIV. 3).

First part of Passage. Two broken blue faience bowls. One shaped like a water-lily leaf and decorated with lotus floral designs (Pl. XLIV. 5), the other of biangular form, with its vertical sides encircled by a band of very indistinct hieroglyphs, which read [hieroglyphs] thus naming the 'Lady of the house Ab-aau' (Pl. XLIV. 4). Near these were three pieces of alabaster making up a complete bowl, a pendant of deep blue glazed faience, some blue glaze inlay, the fore-part of a hippopotamus, a bone and shell necklace, and lastly a leather ball.

---

[1] Found in second sifting.

INTERMEDIATE PERIOD NECROPOLIS

In South Chamber above the Pit. Parts of a bifold wood jewel box (Pl. XLV, the lid was found in the passage), and the following beads and amulets that possibly came out of it:—

A. Blue glaze faience beads imitating shells.
B. Haematite beads and scarab.
C. Cornelian beads.
D. Two amethyst scarabs.
E. A hippopotamus head and crouching monkey in cornelian.
F. Matrix of emerald *Ba*-bird.
G. Necklace of amulets in matrix of emerald, amethyst, cornelian, blue paste, and glazed steatite and faience.

North Chamber above the Pit. A small jewel-box, turned upside down and containing the following ornaments (Pl. XLV. 1 and 2):—

A. Steatite scarab mounted on silver wire.
B. Necklace of small round garnet beads.
C. Garnet and cornelian bracelet.
D. Greenstone cylinder mounted in gold.
E. Broken agate cylinder mounted in gold.
F. Two fragments of nuts of the *Balanites aegyptiaca*.
G. Amulets—cornelian eye, emerald hippopotamus head, silver plaque, and gold bead.
H. A tiny string of gold, silver, cornelian, and turquoise beads of the most minute and exquisite workmanship.

Nearly every basket of earth from the floor of this tomb contained numbers of deep violet lozenge-shaped ornaments made of glazed pottery. They are peculiar to the XIIth Dynasty, and seemingly were used for decorating the wrappings of the mummy, as is well illustrated by a mask cartonnage found in tomb No. 25, where they are depicted in rows and forming part of an ornamentation (Pl. XLIV. 2). In some cases actual mummy-cloth was found adhering to them, and all had some adhesive substance on their backs.

A complete series of pottery belonging to this tomb is given in Pl. XLVII, Figs. 1 and 2.

Fig. 1. A. Rough red pottery, coloured red, with white band.
B.   ,,   ,,   with white spots.
C.   ,,   ,,   coloured red with white stripes.
D.   ,,   ,,   rim and neck coloured red.
E. Fine red pottery, plain.
F. Grey pottery, with 〰 ⚬ written in red upon it.
G. Pink pottery, plain.
H. Grey pottery, ornamented with black, red, and yellow drop pattern.
I. Very fine terra-cotta pottery, plain.

Fig. 1. J. Fine red pottery, coloured red or terra-cotta.
K. Soft red pottery, plain.
L and N. Fine red pottery, with rims coloured red.
M. Fine red pottery, with white surface.

Fig. 2 illustrates two trays divided into compartments and two small vases, made of a very coarse red pottery.

Botanical specimens found in this tomb are figured in Pl. LXXIX. 2 under the letters A and H. The latter, a stone fruit, was found in great quantities, as well as frequently in the other tombs that were opened.

Pit Tomb No. 25.

A pit tomb partially concealed by the paving-blocks of the terrace colonnade and foundations of the north boundary wall of the temple.

In the upper rubbish filling the pit were bricks from the doorway and broken pottery, giving evidence of former riflers; and, after a descent of some three metres or more, the openings of the sepulchral vaults at either side were exposed. These chambers, half-filled with earth that had poured in from the shaft, had in them remains of coffins, oblong in form, broken, and ant-eaten. They were of plain, thick wood, without decorations, and only the inner shell had, in some cases, bands of inscription. In the shaft itself, at the bottom, was a single coffin, dragged out from one of the chambers at the time of the early violation.

At first this grave seemed to be a great disappointment. But when, in Lord Carnarvon's presence, the men found in the lower filling of the shaft an ivory pin and a piece of a box with silver binding[1], our hopes were raised. Lord Carnarvon at once stopped the workmen until a time when full surveillance of the clearing could be made. It was a difficult job, most careful work had to be done with trowel, bellows, and sometimes a spoon, extricating fragile objects while stones and sand poured down from the overhanging masonry above in a menacing manner at every gust of wind.

On the following day operations were begun by clearing the bottom steps of the shaft and searching the coffin. Under the latter, nine more ivory pins, fragments of alabaster, cosmetic vases, the broken parts of an ebony and cedar-wood toilet-box inlaid with ivory, and fragments of an ornamented ivory gaming-board were discovered, twisted and shattered into a hundred pieces. The coffin, too far gone for us to hope to preserve it (ants having eaten the whole of the wood, leaving only the bitumen coating perforated and like an eggshell), had had bands of yellow hieroglyphs along its sides and ends; but only here and there could a few signs be discerned. Still, enough could be made out to trace the title and name 'Great one of the southern tens, Rensenb' (which was afterwards

[1] This was part of the toilet-box, Pls. XLVIII–IX.

corroborated by the inscription on the mirror handle found on the mummy), and certain of the hieroglyphs were of the 'mutilated' type (i. e. 🦅 for 🦅, and 〜 for 〜) often found in texts of the late XIIth Dynasty and Intermediate Period.[1]

The mummy, lying on its side, was reduced to a black powder through spontaneous combustion, caused by the damp that had filtered through from above. It had a cartonnage mask covering the head and shoulders, with gilt face, the head-dress painted yellow and striated with grey-green bands which had oval spots in black (illustrating the use of the violet ornaments found in tomb No. 24). Embedded in the wrappings, at the small of the back, was a blue faience hippopotamus (Pl. LI. 1). Round the neck a gold and obsidian necklace and a 'Shen' brooch of gold and cornelian (Pl. LI. 2). On the breast, concealed in the linen wrappings, was a bronze mirror with ebony handle mounted and inlaid with gold. The inscription upon it reads 〜 𓊃𓈖𓂋 'Great one of the southern tens, Rensenb, repeating life' (Pl. LI. 2). How it came about that these chambers should be ravaged, this burial dragged into the daylight of the open shaft, and yet unrifled, is a mystery yet to be solved.

In the Southern Chamber. At the entrance were the front part and pieces of the drawer of the toilet-box (Pl. XLVIII. 1), three alabaster vase lids, an alabaster vase, and a gold bead. Besides these articles this chamber had planks from wooden canopies and coffins, and the remains of three mummies (one a child) charred to soot. In the depression in the floor and lower chamber were found two broken ivory crocodiles, two splinters of a mystic wand, and the body of a stripped mummy; under the latter, in the dust, were beads of a necklace.

In the North Chamber. Among the many parts of coffins was one bearing inscriptions giving the usual prayers, &c., for a certain lady named 𓊃𓏏 'Henut', born of 𓈖𓏏 'Sent'. Here were also despoiled mummies, one of them having a wig of plaited hair (decayed), clasped by a gold fillet, and a necklace. Some stray beads and a mud sealing bearing a coil pattern were found when sifting the lower layer of dust covering the floor.

The following paragraphs give details of the objects found in this tomb that are not fully described above, including the pottery found scattered in its different chambers.

Toilet-box (Pls. XLVIII–XLIX). An oblong box, made of cedar wood, veneered with ebony and ivory, and measuring 28·5 × 18 × 20 cms.

The front, two sides, end, and lid have in their centres large slabs of ivory, bordered by two narrow strips of ebony and ivory, with broad margins of ebony, the whole giving a unique appearance. The front is made to pull forward, and has attached to it a drawer half the depth and the whole length of the box

---

[1] See Coffin-tomb No. 27.

(see Fig. 1, Pl. XLVIII). This drawer has its edges, top and bottom, veneered with thin strips of ivory, glued to its solid ebony sides and end, and in it a shelf, made of two pieces of wood, pierced with eight holes to receive vases for cosmetics and other toilet requisites.[1] The drawer slides in beneath a tray attached to the inner walls of the box. Access to the tray can only be obtained by raising the lid of the box; and it has, besides two small partitions in the corner, a hollow scooped out of the bottom to receive a mirror (see Fig. 2, Pl. XLVIII).[2]

The lid and front have silver knobs let into bindings of the same metal.

Engraved upon the front ivory slab is a delightful little scene (Pl. XLIX. 1) of the owner, ⌒𓅓𓏛 'Kemen', 𓊹𓏺 'true Royal friend', ⌒ 'whom he (the king) loves', 𓃀𓏺𓂸 'Chief over the secrets of the Royal mouth', 𓃉𓆼𓏺𓏛 'the keeper of the department of the kitchen', offering to his lord, the King Amenemhat IV. Around the margin of the top of the lid, gravered and inlaid with ivory powder is an inscription (Pl. XLIX. 2) bearing the prenomen and nomen of Amenemhat IV, with a religious formula to 'Sebek' ⌒𓃀𓏺 Lord of Illahun (in the Fayûm) that he may give a good burial and long service to the ka of Kemen. The legend here gives also the name of Kemen's mother 𓃀𓏛𓏺 'Ana'. The method adopted in the construction of the box is so peculiar that it is worth particular notice. Each front, side, end, and lid is made of six pieces of cedar wood, viz. a centre panel to receive the large slab of ivory, on either side two thin slips to receive the narrow strips of ebony and ivory, and lastly a top and bottom rail for the broad ebony margins. In fact, the cedarwood body is made of as many pieces as there are horizontal overlaying leaves of the superior materials, all of which, with the exception of the front, where dowels are introduced, were merely stuck together by glue. The corners of the box are mitred, and the ends of the drawer dovetailed to the body of the front part of the box.

The four alabaster vases (Pl. LII. 1) belong to the drawer; there were three fragments of others.

Ivory Gaming-board[3] (Pl. L). Shaped like an axe blade and resting on four bull's legs carved in solid ivory. The dimensions are 15 × 10 cms. (maximum measurement), total height 7 cms.

It contains a small drawer of ivory and ebony, which has a bolt of ivory shot in copper staples for fixing it when closed. Belonging to the game are ten carved ivory pins or playing pieces—five have dogs' heads, and five jackals' heads; these, no doubt, were kept in the drawer.

---

[1] In the Cairo Museum eight similar vases belonging to a toilet-box bear the names of sacred oils, Nos. 18652–8.

[2] In the Cairo Museum is a wooden tray for mirror with two hollows or receptacles for materials for polishing (?) mirror face, No. 44012.

[3] Petrie, *Kahun, Gurob and Hawara*, Pl. XVI, p. 30, a similar gaming-board in pottery.

Its construction is a flat top made of two ivory slabs, backed by two wooden panels which are joined together by three transverse wood pegs passed through the thickness of each panel. The bottom was made of one piece of wood with crossbars at either end. The curved ivory sides and end are backed with blocks of wood that take the same shape as the board, and leave in the interior an oblong space to allow entry of the drawer. The ivory bull's legs are tongued into the wooden side-blocks, and are held there by means of three ebony rivets. Round the four edges, top and bottom, as well as the four corners, was an ebony veneer, most of which was destroyed. Glue was the means of adhesion. The wood used was sycamore. The upper surface (Pl. L. 1) has engraved upon it a palm-tree

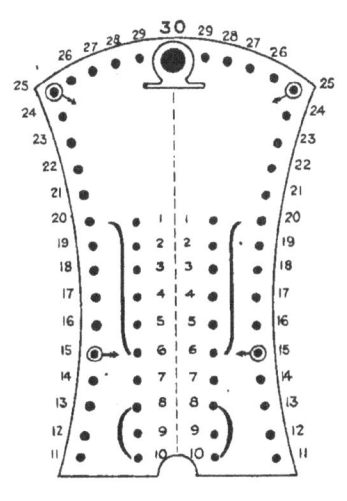

FIG. 14. KEY TO GAMING-BOARD.

surmounted by the sign 'Shen' (see Fig. 14), the latter being pierced through the ivory and wooden body beneath. On each side of the palm-stem is a parallel line of ten holes, along the edges of the two sides a row of fifteen holes, and at the top edge on either side of the 'Shen' a row of four holes (and if including the corner hole, five). Each hole is encircled by a small ring, engraved, and is pierced through the ivory and wood below, and these holes were intended to receive the playing pieces. For some reason or other, a large hole was made in the centre of the palm-tree, but it was afterwards filled in. In the front edge of the board is a small semicircular notch, made to permit the thumb to grip the drawer when opening it.

Now a word as to the game itself; how was it played, and how were the moves denoted? Presuming the 'Shen' sign, which forms a large centre hole at the top, to be the goal, we find on either side twenty-nine holes, or including the goal, thirty aside. Among these holes, on either side, two are marked $\underset{\circ}{\mathring{\mathrm{I}}}$ *nefer*, 'good'; and four others are linked together by curved lines (see Fig. 14). Assuming that the holes marked 'good' incur a gain, it would appear that the others, connected by lines, incur a loss. Taking this for granted, and that the play terminates at the goal 'Shen', the game seems then to commence at the heart of the palm—the only place where five playing pieces aside could be placed without clashing with the obstacles (i. e. holes incurring gain or loss). Thus, starting from the first hole under the palm, and calling it No. 1, the tenth hole, by the indicating lines, shows a forfeit of two points, and the twentieth hole a forfeit of fourteen points. The good holes Nos. 15 and 25 have nothing to indicate what gain was attached to them. If it should be a profit of a certain number of holes, one would expect to find them marked like the forfeits, but possibly it was that they entitled (?) the player to the right of a second move, which could not be marked in such a manner. Now the moves themselves could easily have been denoted by the chance cast of knuckle-bones or dice,[1] both being known to the ancient Egyptians at an early period; and if so we have before us a simple, but exciting, game of chance, 'Hounds contra Jackals', and played somewhat as follows:—The opponents, taking each a side, place their five men in holes Nos. 1 to 5,[2] under the palm. The hounds having obtained the right of first throw, by a toss or some equivalent, start:—

	HOUNDS.			JACKALS.	
1st H.	Cast 3	= hole 8	1st J.	Cast 6	= hole 11
,,	1	= ,, 9	,,	5	= ,, 16
,,	5	= ,, 14	,,	3	= ,, 19
,,	3	= ,, 17	,,	6 = 25, wins 2nd throw = 4	= ,, 29
,,	6	= ,, 23	,,	6 Returns to 25, wins 2nd throw 4	= ,, 29
,,	4	= ,, 27	,,	6 Returns to 25, wins 2nd throw 1	= ,, 26
,,	3 = the goal	= ,, 30	,,	3	= ,, 29

1 point to Hds. (winning piece remains in goal).   Jks. lose their piece.

---

[1] For knuckle-bones see group No. 25, tomb No. 37. Cp. Quibell, *Excavations Saqqara*, p. 114, Pl. LXIII. Dice: I have found three specimens among objects from the rubbish heaps of the temple of Dêr el Bahari, and as there were no antiquities here that could be later than the XVIIIth Dynasty, one is led to suppose that the dice are of the same date. Two of the dice were of clay and one was made of limestone.

[2] For the numerical order of the holes see Fig. 14. Only one piece aside can be played at a time, as if more they might win the same hole and hence clash; and only one die used.

INTERMEDIATE PERIOD NECROPOLIS

HOUNDS.		JACKALS.	
2nd H. Cast 4	= hole 8	*2nd J.* Cast 3	= hole 7
,, 6	= ,, 14	,, 4	= ,, 11
,, 5	= ,, 19	,, 5	= ,, 16
,, 1 = 20, forfeit 14	= ,, 6	,, 5	= ,, 21
,, 4 = 10, forfeit 2	= ,, 8	,, 6	= ,, 27
,, 5	= ,, 13	,, 4 Returns to	= ,, 29
,, 6	= ,, 19	,, 4 Returns to	= ,, 27
,, 3	= ,, 22	,, 3 = the goal	= ,, 30
Hds. lose their piece.		*1 point to Jks.* (winning piece remains in goal).	
3rd H. Cast 6	= hole 9	*3rd J.* Cast 5	= hole 8
,, 6 = 15, win 2nd throw 6	= ,, 21	,, 4	= ,, 12
,, 6	= ,, 27	,, 6	= ,, 18
,, 5 Returns to	= ,, 28	,, 6	= ,, 24
,, 4 Returns to	= ,, 28	,, 6 = the goal	= ,, 30
Hds. lose their piece.		*2 points to Jks.* (winning pieces remain in goal).	
4th H. Cast 3	= hole 5	*4th J.* Cast 2	= hole 4
,, 4	= ,, 9	,, 3	= ,, 7
,, 4	= ,, 13	,, 3 = 10, forfeits 2	= ,, 8
,, 7 = 20, forfeits 14	= ,, 6	,, 4	= ,, 12
,, 3	= ,, 9	,, 6	= ,, 18
,, 5	= ,, 14	,, 3	= ,, 21
,, 2	= ,, 16	,, 2	= ,, 23
,, 4 = 20, forfeits 14	= ,, 6	,, 5	= ,, 28
,, 6	= ,, 12	,, 1	= ,, 29
,, 2	= ,, 14	,, 5 Returns to	= ,, 26
,, 5	= ,, 19	,, 4 = the goal	= ,, 30
Hds. lose their piece.		*3 points to Jks.* (winning pieces remain in goal).	
5th H. Cast 2	= hole 3	*5th J.* Cast 5	= hole 6
,, 4	= ,, 7	,, 5	= ,, 11
,, 5	= ,, 12	,, 4 = 15, wins 2nd throw 1	= ,, 16
,, 2	= ,, 14	,, 6	= ,, 22
,, 6 = 20, forfeits 14	= ,, 6	,, 1	= ,, 23
,, 4 = 10, forfeits 2	= ,, 8	,, 4	= ,, 27
,, 6	= ,, 14	,, 6 Returns to	= ,, 27
,, 1 = 15, wins 2nd throw = 6	= ,, 21	,, 2	= ,, 29
,, 4 = 25, wins 2nd throw = 5 = the goal	= ,, 30	,, 4 Returns to	= ,, 27
2 points to Hds.		Jks. lose their man, but have 3 men in the goal, and thus win by 1 point.	

Necklace. Of long drop-shaped beads made of gold and three kinds of coloured stones—cornelian, lapis lazuli, and matrix of emerald. They were strung in the ancient colour order, viz. red, blue, yellow, and green—cornelian for the red, lapis lazuli for the blue, gold for the yellow, and matrix of emerald for the green. Some of the beads had tiny floral tops, which, when combined, formed a lotus column, or perhaps a flower; but by no means did all of them have this additional piece, as was proved by some of the beads still attached by their original threads. Unfortunately this necklace, of exquisite quality, cannot be restrung, as all the wax cores of the gold beads (the gold being only a thin outer covering) has amalgamated, and the holes are completely choked. At present, in their tender state of preservation, to re-bore them would endanger their being split, as some already are.

Amuletic necklace. This second necklace is of quite a different type, very small, and of all kinds of beads and amulets. The order[1] seems to have been alternate groups of barrel garnet beads, divided by minute gold beads, and between them amulets in gold, cornelian, glazed steatite, and faience. There are also tiny cornelian and glaze beads among them. The amulets that occur are the eye, hand, rope-knot, crouching lions, crocodiles, flies, and other strange forms difficult to recognize. The position of these amulets, strung on the necklace, can only be a matter of conjecture.[2]

Shell necklace. Of this only a few pieces were found. They are small shells and ornamental vase-shaped beads, of lapis lazuli, matrix of emerald, and turquoise. Between each was a short cylindrical gold bead.[3]

The obsidian and gold necklace (Pl. LI. 2) hardly requires description, the illustration showing all details. The beads are strung in the exact order in which they were found. The 'Shen' brooch (Pl. LI. 2) was not attached to it.

Pottery. The various types are all shown in Pl. LII. 2.

        A. Soft red pottery.
        B. Fine red pottery.
        C. Rough red pottery.
        D. Rough red pottery with rim coloured red.
        E. Fine red pottery with rim coloured red.
        F. Red pottery.
        G. Red pottery, coloured red.
        H. Rough red pottery spotted white.
        I. Red pottery, coloured red.

Pit Tomb No. 27.

The contents of this tomb (Pl. XXX) were pillaged and almost entirely destroyed, the ants leaving not a fragment of the wood untouched. Among the débris of the original burials was an intrusive one of a child.[4] All that was of importance to record was: (1) A portion of an anthropoid coffin with *Rîshi* decoration, like the case found in Tomb 32 (Pl. LIII. 3), but of much larger

---

[1] This is known by some adhering to one another when found.
[2] See Tomb 24, Pl. XLVI, Fig. 2 G, and amulet necklace of Vth Dynasty, Petrie, *Deshasheh*, Pl. XLVI. This type of necklace seems almost a necessary adjunct to the dead in the earlier periods.
[3] See Tomb 24, Pl. XLVI. A.   [4] See example Pl. LIII. 4.

dimensions and with the face gilt; down the front of this coffin was a vertical inscription, of which the following was visible: [hieroglyphs] naming the 'Scribe of the Army', 'Superintendent of the temple', Nenen...(?); (2) an ear from a silvered mask; (3) three pieces of the upper portion of a stela (the rest of this stela was found in Tomb No. 81, Pl. LIV); (4) a pot (the only one found in the tomb) like Fig. J in Tomb No. 24.

Pit Tomb No. 28.

This grave (Pl. XXX) had even less in it than No. 27; in the shaft was an intrusive burial of a poorish type. The chambers, which were choked with rubbish, contained only a pair of copper forceps, a brown stone bead, and one hydroceramic vase (Pl. LIII. 1).

Pit Tomb No. 29.

This tomb (Pl. XXX) gave access to two other similar graves on either side of it, Nos. 29 A and B. The three were plundered, and their chambers filled with sand almost to the ceiling. In the shaft of No. 29 was a burial with 'dug-out coffin' yielding a scarab, and in its chamber were two other burials, illustrated in Pl. LIII. 4. These were typical examples of the 'dug-out coffin'. They contained 'dried' bodies wrapped in a simple winding-sheet (Intermediate Period?).

No. 29 A. This could not be thoroughly excavated, as the mouth of its shaft was under the southern part of the excavations which has not been cleared, and the sand poured down from above it as fast as it was removed from below, making it too dangerous to clear.

No. 29 B was only accessible through a small hole in the south-west corner of pit No. 29; it gave equal trouble, and could only be excavated under considerable risk, its pit being partially under the foundations of the temple wall. It was full of plundered mummies huddled together under a great weight of sand and stones thrown in by the temple workmen when building the wall. With them was a wooden head-rest, a canopic jar lid, and a scribe's palette, some roughly made chair legs, pieces of cartonnage (of linen covered with plaster, gilt), and a long flexible wooden implement, two metres in length, perhaps a weaver's batten. The types of pottery found in these chambers are shown in Pl. LIII. 5:—

    A. Rough red pottery, decorated with white paint, with holes in the neck for fastening the cover.
    B. Fine red pottery, coloured red.
    C. Red pottery, rim coloured red.
    D. Soft red pottery.
    E. Red pottery, has small spout, and upper part coloured red.
    F. Pink pottery.
    G. Red pottery, rim coloured red.

THE LATE MIDDLE KINGDOM AND

Pit Tombs Nos. 31–34.

This group of tombs (Pl. XXX) is under the Lower Court of the 'Valley'-Temple. The chambers are cut into one another, and thus form a homogeneous series. They were choked up with sand, with but little of their plundered contents left. It was hopeless to try to tell to which of the tombs the few remains belonged, and hence in enumerating them the chamber in which they were found can alone be given.

Pit Tomb No. 31. A 'dug-out' painted coffin burial with roughly painted shawabti box, and the lower portion of the stela found in Tomb No. 27 (Pl. LIV). In its chamber were found a few examples of pottery.

Pit Tomb No. 32. First chamber—an interesting type of a female figure made of painted wood with pottery head.[1] Second chamber—a *Rîshi* coffin (Pl. LIII. 3) belonging (?) to the original burial. It was found lying on its right side in a space on the floor especially cleared for it, and was bound at head and foot with palm fibre cords, which makes it appear to have been re-used. Notwithstanding its appearance of perfect preservation when first discovered, the coffin and even the body inside were so completely rotten that they fell to pieces at the least touch; it was in such a condition that it was impossible to preserve it. It being the most complete mummy case hitherto found in these tombs, a lengthy description is necessary. The case, anthropoid in shape, was decorated as if enveloped by the wings of a bird. This *Rîshi*[2] decoration is on a light yellow ground, the feathers themselves being of deep bluish green, picked out here and there with red and white, and detailed in black. The face was flesh colour, with eyebrows and side-beard straps green, the eye sockets of copper with aragonite eyeballs and obsidian pupils. Down the centre of the front of the coffin was a vertical line of hieroglyphs reading: [hieroglyphs] [*blank space*]. Below the feet are the two kneeling figures of 'Isis' and 'Nephthys' facing one another, and between them a vertical legend reading: [hieroglyphs]

Pit Tomb No. 33. This had nothing in it, and being under the temple construction it was too dangerous to attempt a total clearance of its chamber or chambers.

Pit Tomb No. 34. This had only three intrusive interments, which were in an almost unrecognizable condition. Examples of the pottery vessels scattered about in the chambers of this group are given in Pl. LIII. 2. Their material does not differ from the other examples already described as coming from this necropolis.

The stela of Auy-res (Pl. LIV) found in Tombs No. 27 and 31 is of limestone, measuring 59 × 31 cms.; the inscriptions are incised upon the stone face and

---

[1] See figure found in Tomb No. 54.   [2] Feathered.

INTERMEDIATE PERIOD NECROPOLIS

coloured dark blue; the figures are in the usual colouring and have blue collarettes. The horizontal legend begins with :—

'(1) May the king give an offering to Osiris Khent-amenti, the Great God, Lord of Abydos, that he may give (2) oblations of water, incense, wax, all good and pure things (3) upon which the god lives ... for the ka of the Keeper of the Bow, Auy-res, justified.'

His family are recorded in the following order :—

Row 1. 'His wife, Atef-s-senb.
His son, the Great One of the Southern Tens, Y-meru.
His son. the Great One of the Southern Tens, Erde-en-ptah.

Row 2. His daughter, the servant of the Ruler, Auŷ-senb.
His son, the *Am-khet*,[1] Dedut-res.
His sister, Auŷ-senb.
His son, the *Am-khet*,[1] Y-meru.

Row 3. The Keeper of the Bow, Sa-Hathor.
The Lady, Sent-nw-pw.
The *Uab*-priest of Amen, Sebek-hetep.
The Lady, Sep-en-urdet.'

There was no evidence to show to which of these two tombs this stela belonged.

In the rubbish, and partially under the foundations of the wall of the Lower Court of the 'Valley'-Temple, was a coffin[2] that had been thrown out from one of the XIIth Dynasty tombs. This coffin was of wood, rectangular and oblong in form, with no inscriptions or decoration; it contained a body of a female child. Round her neck was a cornelian necklace still attached by its strings, and on her breast was a bronze mirror reflector; from the manner this reflector was wrapped in linen it must have been buried with the deceased without a handle. The girl's hair was plaited.

Circular Pit No. 35.

This pit (Pl. XXX) was the last and most puzzling of all opened this season. It is a rock-hewn shaft, some three metres in diameter at the mouth and only 63 cms. at the bottom, and thus, like an inverted cone, descends 22·50 metres[3] into the *Tafle* stratum. The filling was absolutely untouched, and from top to bottom consisted of pure black soil from the arable plain; the upper surface had been hardened by water. The bottom of the shaft, apparently unfinished, was on one side slightly deeper than the other. A hollow copper bead-like object of cylindrical-drop shape found on the top surface, was the only object discovered here. At four metres below the surface the shaft had been cut through one of

---

[1] Poulterer (?).   [2] Opposite Tomb No. 27.
[3] 22·50 metres = 74 ft. approximate.

the pit tombs¹ of the cemetery, and the hole in the side thus caused had been mended with mud bricks. Its whole meaning is at present inexplicable.²

No. 36, Pl. XXX.

A large mud-brick structure of which only part of one side has been exposed by our excavations. This part lies within the area of the 'Valley'-Temple (No. 14), and is in line with the Colonnaded Terrace. The one end (north-east corner) and the stretch of some thirty-five metres of wall that has been uncovered does not give us enough data to tell its exact meaning or date. It is built upon the bed-rock, and it averages four metres in height. The brickwork seems to be earlier than that of the New Kingdom. The probabilities are that it belongs to the Intermediate Period or even perhaps the Middle Kingdom. Towards the southern end of the part cleared by us the foundation of the wall has been built over the courtyard of Tomb No. 41.

Tomb No. 37.

This tomb, shaped like an inverted T, is the largest one yet opened in this group; in fact it could be ranked among the larger mausolea of the Theban Necropolis, and evidently belonged to one of the higher Egyptian dignitaries (Pls. XXX, LV).

It consists of (1) a long corridor having an eastern frontage with some eighteen openings, which give access to a rock-cutting of the nature of an open court. (2) Cut in the back wall of this corridor, and at right angles to it, are a long central subterranean passage leading to a hall (C), and two sepulchral chambers. Access to one of these sepulchral chambers (J) is by means of a staircase, while the other (E) is approached by a vertical pit (D) of four metres in depth; both are cut in the floor of the hall (C). The northern end of the corridor was divided off by a stone and mortar partition, with a small chamber (B) at the back, which was presumably a portion divided off for a member of the owner's family. The blind end of the corridor on the south had originally been closed by a mud-brick wall, and no doubt thus formed another private compartment like the third chamber (A), which is parallel to the central passage.

It appears, therefore, that there were five distinct burial chambers (and if counting the hall (C) a sixth) which were closed, leaving the greater part of the corridor and central passage open for any ceremonial rites that might be made by the living relations in favour of the deceased.

This great tomb, dating from the Late Middle Kingdom, was found to have been utilized for the storing of numerous stray burials of epochs ranging through the Intermediate Period down to the early part of the XVIIIth Dynasty. Our reasons for assigning this date to the tomb were the antiquities (Nos. 85, 86, 87)

---

[1] Not numbered or excavated yet.
[2] It has been suggested that it was made for a tree, but no vegetable remains were found here, and it seems too deep for such a purpose.

INTERMEDIATE PERIOD NECROPOLIS

found in the layer of rubbish and burnt ashes that covered its floors; these were quite distinct from the coffins and other antiquities forming the cache which rested upon the rubbish.

It is difficult to imagine how such a large mausoleum, cut in the shallow and crumbling limestone stratum, with so many openings, could for long have been protected from plunderers. The smoke-blackened walls show how its contents were destroyed, and the martins' nests, together with the innumerable mason-bee cells that adhered to the walls and ceiling, show that the tomb had been left open after having been plundered for a lengthy period, before it was re-used as a storehouse.

When revealed, the main entrance was not closed by bricks or by stones, as was often the custom, but the sand was merely poured over when the Ancients last covered it up. The remaining openings had certainly in some instances been closed by planks from old coffins, but the greater number were carelessly filled like the entrance. Three of the inner chambers were carefully closed; in two cases with bricks, and in one with stones. These closed chambers were as follows:—

Hall (*C*) had its doorway bricked two-thirds up with crude mud-bricks and *Tafle* mortar, and the remaining third of its opening with similar bricks but with a mud mortar (Pl. LVI), showing that it had been opened and reclosed a second time. The mortar-bed of mud for this last closing was found in the central passage (Pls. LV, LVI. 14) just as it was left by the ancient mason.

Chamber (*A*) had its doorway completely closed with flat mud-bricks, and the outer surface smeared over with *Tafle* stucco (Pl. LVII, above the coffin to the left), which was stamped in numerous places with a seal giving the *Nebti* name ( ) of Thothmes I (see Pl. LVIII. 1).

Chamber (*B*) had its entrance blocked by a heap of stones piled before it and a coffin placed in front (Pl. LIX. 1).

Behind these bricked-up doorways was the greater mass of the burials that were stored in the tomb.

From whence all these burials came we have no evidence to show us at present, nor can we tell for certain the reason for their being concealed in this particular tomb. It is possible that, while clearing the ground for the great dromos of Dêr el Bahari, and during the preparation of its 'Valley'-Temple, stray interments were disturbed, and that this tomb being so situated that it must necessarily be covered by the 'Valley'-Temple, it was used by the pious officials of the Theban Necropolis as a place of concealment (see position of tomb in relation to the temple, Pl. XXX).

The seal impressions stamped upon the wall that closed chamber (*A*), we have just seen, give the *Nebti* name of Thothmes I, and thus we have a date for the time when some of the coffins were re-interred, and probably the date when the above monument must have been begun.

The scattered manner in which the coffins were placed in the different

K

chambers and passages of the tomb, and the fact that one of the chambers (*C*) had been re-opened and re-closed, tends to show that they were not placed in the tomb at one time, which is in favour of the theory that they really were disturbed interments stored there from time to time during the course of some work.

The latest date found among the objects of the whole cache was Thothmes III, and that name occurred only on one object—a small scarab (Pl. LXXII. 58 from burial No. 53, p. 80).

The two chambers in the corridor (*A*, *B*) contained eight and four separate coffins respectively; the hall (*C*) at the end of the passage had fourteen; in the pit (*D*), piled from bottom to top, were eighteen cases; and in the bottom crypt (*E*) was another batch of eight sarcophagi. Thus, counting also those lying about the open corridor and passage which numbered twelve, we obtain a total of sixty-four coffins. Besides these there were also twenty-eight other objects pertaining to funeral equipments.

Among these sixty-four miscellaneous wooden sarcophagi, some containing as many as four mummies in each, there were seven distinct types, and with them a great number of children's coffins.

The types of the coffins of adults were: (1) Decorated rectangular, (2) plain rectangular, (3) 'dug-out', (4) *Ríshi*, (5) plain anthropoid, (6) semi-decorated anthropoid, and (7) decorated anthropoid of the New Kingdom. Each of these groups I have treated below, followed by a separate detailed description of each burial and object found in the tomb (see p. 70).

Decorated rectangular coffins, Nos. 7, 35, 59, 63 (for examples see Pl. LX. 1). The coffins of this class are most probably contemporaneous with the Hyksos period. They are similar to the coffin in the Cairo Museum belonging to a certain Abdu, a contemporary of the last of the Hyksos kings.[1] Coffin No. 59 (p. 81) contained four mummies, two of which, and a basket containing a scarab, gave conflicting evidence to the above dating. The scarabs found on these two mummies bear the names of Thothmes I and II (Pl. LXXII. 59 A, D), and the one in the basket (Pl. LXXII. 59) according to Newberry is of a similar date. But the remaining antiquities, i.e. head-rest, biangular bowl, and black vase of foreign character (Pl. LXVIII. 59) may be of an earlier period, and perhaps belonged to one of the other two mummies found in this coffin, and to the original interment. Coffin No. 63 (p. 82), which contained two mummies, had somewhat similar objects (Pl. LXVIII. 63) to No. 59, but on one of the mummies, a woman, there were two cowroids (Pl. LXXII. 63 A) which could be referred to the Early XVIIIth Dynasty. No. 7 (p. 70) yielded nothing beyond the actual body, and gives no further help for or against dating this group to these Dynasties.

Plain rectangular coffins. Of these coffins there are three kinds, those with gable tops, those with flat tops, and those with open-grid bottoms (for examples see Pl. LX. 2). The gable-topped coffins, Nos. 53, 62, 64, 65, 69, 71, 77, 83, with

---

[1] Maspero, *Guide C. M.*, 1911, pp. 386, 510, and Lacau, *Cat. Gen. C. M.*, No. 28108.

lids sometimes nearly semicircular in section, have always on the lid a longitudinal beam in the centre. These are probably of the same epoch as the other two kinds, but I am treating them here separately; they are very similar to some described by M. Lacau as *Sarcophages antérieurs au Nouvel Empire* in his catalogue of that section of the Cairo Museum, more especially to No. 28030, which has exactly the same central beam and construction of lid. One is thus led to believe them to be of this period. Groups of objects found in some of them (for examples see Pl. LXIX. 64, 71, and 83) could be anterior to the New Kingdom. On the other hand, Nos. 53 and 62 (Pls. LXIX. 58 and LXXII. 62 A, B) contained antiquities of the Early XVIIIth Dynasty to as late as the time of Princess Neferu-ra (Hatshepsût's daughter) and Thothmes III (see Pl. LXXII. 53). This last evidence is not absolutely contradictory, for we have examples of rectangular wooden coffins belonging to the New Kingdom. I am inclined, however, to assume that they have been re-used in these particular instances. No. 83 of the batch (p. 86) was covered intentionally with stone chippings and placed in a niche (Pl. LV. G) especially made for it. This gave us every reason to suppose it to be a burial made in the tomb when left open after destruction, and before it was used as a storehouse. The three pots (Pl. LXXIV. G) belonging to this coffin, and carefully placed behind it, give us a clue to the date of the stray pottery found mingled with the other coffins and lying on the floors of the passage and chambers of this great tomb, namely, the Intermediate Period.

The flat-topped coffins, Nos. 8, 15, 21, 22, 34, 36, 46, 48, 49, 55, 57, 75, 76, 78, 79, and 81 were often found to be made of scrap timber from other sarcophagi, and on the whole they perhaps incline to be later than the gable-topped coffins. The latest fixed date found on the objects in them was that of the Divine Wife, Hatshepsût, which occurred in that of No. 21, on a silver-mounted scarab ring (Pl. LXXII. 21). A head-rest found with it is certainly different in character to others found here, and it has engraved upon its stem the deities Bes and Taurt (Pl. LXVIII. 21). The head-rest found in coffin No. 57 (Pl. LXVIII. 57) has a short base, and it strikes one as being of a character between the earlier long-based types like No. 15 (Pl. LXVIII. 15) and that of No. 21. Burial No. 78 was furnished with the most complete group of objects (Pl. LXVIII. 78), and might be referred to the Early XVIIIth Dynasty. The last section of this group, the open-grid bottomed coffins, Nos. 50 and 52, are of smaller size (see Pl. LX. 52). They recall some of the older coffins of the Early Middle Kingdom found at Aswân that have false bottoms of lattice work.[1] But these coffins constructed out of wood from older sarcophagi are seemingly later than the rest, for in one of them, No. 50, a necklace of beads and amulets (Pl. LXXIII. 50) is certainly of the beginning of the XVIIIth Dynasty.

---

[1] *Annales*, 1903, Tome IV, p. 70. A coffin of a certain Heq-Tau. 'The bottom of the coffin is divided into small compartments by a kind of wooden frame or trellis, each division being filled with earth, probably representing cultivated land.'

'Dug-out' coffins. Nos. 37 and 58 (see Pl. LXI. 58) are exceedingly rough, and cut out of tree trunks. One of them had its lid bound to its shell with rope. From a scarab (Pl. LXXII. 37) found in coffin 37 these 'Dug-outs' seem to belong to the beginning of the Second Theban Empire, though similar specimens found in some of the tombs recorded above were of a slightly earlier date.

Ríshi coffins. Nos. 2, 10, 11, 12, 60, 66, and 70 are a type peculiar to the Theban Necropolis, and only a limited number of these coffins have been discovered. They are named *Ríshi*[1] from the design painted upon them being composed of two large wings of many-coloured feathers that envelop the mummy form; for examples of those found here, see Pl. LXII. 1.[2] They belong to the Intermediate Period. With the seven specimens discovered in this cache there were only a few beads, a cowroid seal (Pl. LXXII. 11), a bronze mirror, and a wooden head-rest (Pl. LXX. 70); and, with the exception of the cowroid seal which might be as late as the Early XVIIIth Dynasty, these objects do not seem later than the end of the Intermediate Period.

The richest interment of this type, in personal objects, was the one found by Prof. Petrie,[3] and the antiquities here were all characteristic of the time between the Middle Kingdom and the New Empire.

If one compares the facial type of these coffins, more especially the profiles, of all the examples known, it will be noticed (as Erskine Nicol pointed out to me) that they have a distinct and uniform character. And it is not without interest to note that the expression and peculiarity of face strongly resembles the so-called Hyksos heads discovered by Prof. Naville at Bubastis.[4]

Plain anthropoid coffins, Nos. 5, 29, 38, and 47 (Pl. LXI. 29). Only one coffin of this series contained any material that was of use for dating. This coffin, No. 47 (p. 79), with the mummy of a woman, had a scarab of the Hyksos Period, a cowroid in glass, and a glazed scaraboid bead of the Second Theban Empire (see Pl. LXXII. 47). The two latter objects plainly show that the burial cannot be anterior to the Early XVIIIth Dynasty.

Semi-decorated anthropoid coffins, Nos. 6 and 68 (Pl. LXI. 6). These two specimens form a small group of their own. They are of very coarse workmanship, in design resembling those of the New Kingdom, but in the face they have a likeness to the *Ríshi* type. They bear no names or inscriptions, and the only objects beside the mummies found in them were a few bead-bangles (Pl. LXXIII. 6), which give but little help towards their date. One is inclined to believe that they are coffins of the poorer people of the Early New Empire.

Decorated anthropoid coffins of the New Kingdom, Nos. 23, 24, 73, and 74 (Pls. LXII. 73, LXIII. 74). These coffins are painted white and embellished

---

[1] An Arabic expression introduced by Vassalli.
[2] See specimen, Mariette's *Monuments divers*, Pl. LI, coffin of Aqhor. Another specimen was found in Tomb 27 in 1910 (Pl. LIII. 3).
[3] Petrie, *Qurneh*, 1909, pp. 6-9, Pls. XXII-XXIX.
[4] Naville, *Bubastis*, 1887-9, and Petrie, *History of Egypt*, I, Figs. 142-3.

with a light and simple decoration. The finest specimen of the series was No. 23 (p. 74), but unfortunately it was found in very bad preservation, the rock ceiling of the tomb having fallen upon it. Coffin No. 24 (p. 74) contained, besides other antiquities, two scarabs of a much earlier period than the date of the coffin; one was of the XIIIth Dynasty and bears the name of a 'Herald' Ren-senb, the other is of the Intermediate Period and bears an enigmatical inscription (Pl. LXXII. 24). In coffin No. 73 (p. 84) was a small pot containing a kind of pomatum, which shows the use of such small pottery vessels so frequently found with burials of this cache. Coffin No. 74 (p. 85, Pl. LXIII) was of particular interest, it having depicted upon its sides, in place of the usual representations of the gods, scenes of burial ceremonies; and among the formulae written upon it occurs a variant form of the sign for Horus.[1]

A fifth coffin, No. 18 (Pl. LXII. 18), of simple blue decoration upon a white ground, might be placed in the same category, though perhaps it is of a slightly earlier date than the above four.

Two viscera boxes, Nos. 19 and 20, found at the feet of coffins 23 and 24, probably belong to them. One of the boxes, No. 20 (p. 73, Pl. LXI. 20), bore the name Ta-nezem, which occurred on coffin No. 24. At the feet of coffins 73 and 74 was another viscera box, No. 72.

Children's coffins. These numerous small coffins were of exceedingly rough workmanship, without any decoration, and were of the following types: (1) Rectangular (Pl. LXI. 61, 80), (2) 'dug-out' rectangular (Pl. LXI. 41), (3) 'dug-out' anthropoid (No. 40), and (4) a type peculiar to itself (Pl. LXI. 42). No doubt their parents were among the many adult burials found in this cache, but we have nothing to tell us to which they belong. One of these small coffins, No. 84, had a small necklace (Pl. LXXIII. 84) like that found in 1910 in the Middle Empire tomb No. 24 (p. 53, Pl. XLV. H). Another, No. 31, contained (resting upon the shins of a mummy of a small child) a basket with the different kinds of necklaces represented in Pl. LXXIII under No. 31.[2] On one of these necklaces a bead, cowroid in shape, bore the prenomen of Thothmes I. These necklaces did not appear to belong to the child, as a number of stone chippings were found mingled with them, which would suggest their having been gathered up from the ground and thrown into the coffin.

The method used in wrapping the mummies was found in general to be similar in all cases. They had always one shroud of linen laid over them, and sometimes one underneath, with an occasional one between the actual bindings of the body. The limbs were separately bound. In some instances the mummy was tied up with long twisted linen ropes bound round, spirally, from head to foot, and these, I believe, had been re-wrapped. Some of the mummies were bitumenized.

---

[1] My attention was drawn to this fact by Professor Spiegelberg.

[2] The three examples given in this illustration are the types found among the many necklaces belonging to the basket that was found lying in the coffin.

In the *Rishi* burials the fashion adopted closely resembled the *Rishi* interment discovered by Professor Petrie (Petrie, *Qurneh*, pp. 7-9).

The scarabs found on the mummies, when worn as a ring, were always placed on the third finger of the left hand. A few beads sprinkled among the wrappings of the body was also found to be a not uncommon custom.

Among other objects pertaining to the funeral equipments found in this cache there were: No. 16, a rush-work basket containing articles of toilet use, and a scarab of Amenhetep I (Pls. LXIV, LXV. 16); No. 25, another similar basket containing what appears to be part of a scribe's outfit (Pl. LXVI). Here a reed-case and palette illustrates the hieroglyph, but unfortunately the small bladder for colour, shown in the centre of the sign, is missing in this case. Nos. 28, 63 A, and 92, musical instruments (Pl. LXXI); No. 28, a bird trap (Pl. LXIV); Nos. 26, 28, two writing tablets; and Nos. 88, 89, and 90, three panel stelae (Pls. LXXV to LXXVIII).

Catalogue of the Antiquities found in Tomb No. 37.[1]

Entrance.

1. A bunch of vine leaves and twigs lying upon the débris of the tomb.

North Wing.

2. *Rishi coffin.* Shell, cut out of a stem of a tree, and left quite plain and rough. Lid, painted detail and feathering like No. 66, but in this case painted upon a yellow ground only. It bears no inscriptions, and the face is coloured yellow (Pls. LVII, LXII. 2).

Contents:—A well-preserved mummy of a tall man.

3. A very decayed mummy of a man, wrapped in a mat and bound with cord.

4. A group of broken pots and some vine leaves.

5. *Plain anthropoid coffin.* Like No. 29, but has its face painted yellow.

Contents:—A mummy of an old woman very loosely wrapped.

6. *Semi-decorated anthropoid coffin.* Lid and shell painted white with longitudinal and transverse bands in yellow. Face yellow. Head-dress yellow with blue lines. It bears no inscriptions (Pls. LIX, LXI. 6).

Contents:—Three mummies covered with a shroud. Two were lying side by side, the third was reversed with its head towards the feet of the others. (*a*) The reversed burial, mummy of a woman re-wrapped; (*b*) mummy of a woman; (*c*) mummy of a man with bead bangles on left wrist, the beads were of dark violet glaze (Pl. LXXIII. 6).

7. *Decorated rectangular coffin.* The general ground colour is yellow, and the design painted upon it is in red, green, dark blue, and white. On the ends, the figures of *Isis* and *Nephthys* kneeling upon *neb* signs are

[1] For the actual positions of the objects refer to plan of tomb, Pl. LV.

North Wing (continued).

depicted upon a white ground. The lid was tied on with ropes of Dôm palm-fibre (Pl. LX. 7).

Contents:—Mummy of an old man, reduced to a mere skeleton. Among the débris from the abdomen of the mummy was a bladder-stone.

8. *Plain rectangular flat-topped coffin.* Similar to No. 75.

Contents:—Mummy of a man covered with a sheet. Resting against the coffin was an earthenware pot (Pl. LXXIV. 8).

Central passage.

9. The base of a wooden head-rest (this was similar to those found in the coffins of this cache).

10. *Rishi coffin.* Broken and in bad condition. It was made and decorated like No. 2.

Contents:—Mummy of a man very roughly wrapped.

11. *Rishi coffin.* Shell, plain wood. Lid, the ground colour white and yellow, and the detail like No. 66. The longitudinal band for text down the front had no inscription (Pls. LVI, LXII. 11).

Contents:—Mummy of a woman lying flat on its back with the head turned towards the left. A small child's mummy was resting on her feet. Among the débris at the bottom of the coffin were: (1) a few small beads of greenish blue faience; (2) a cowroid seal of green glazed steatite (Pl. LXXII. 11); in the hole pierced through the cowroid seal were remains of thread.

12. *Rishi coffin.* Like No. 66 (Pl. LVI. 12).

Contents:—A scantily wrapped mummy of a man.

13. *The frame of a wooden stool.* This was leaning against the wall, and it rested upon the mutilated remains of a mummy (Pl. LVI. 13). With the débris of the mummy was (1) the greater portion of a large necklace of blue faience beads: the remainder of this necklace was found scattered upon the floor as far as the entrance of the hall at the end of the central passage (Pl. LXXIII. 13); (2) the mouth and nose of a mummy mask.

14. *A mortar-bed.* The mud mortar here (Pl. LVI. 14) appears to have been mixed for the second closing of the doorway of the hall (*C*); the first closing of this doorway was with a *Tafle* mortar.

15. *Plain rectangular flat-topped coffin.* Like No. 75, the coffin shows signs of rough handling, and had been broken to pieces.

Contents:—Mummy of a woman. By the left shoulder was a wooden head-rest broken into two pieces and the central portion of its stem missing (Pl. LXVIII. 15); on the third finger of the left hand was a blue glazed steatite scarab tied with string (Pl. LXXII. 15); and sprinkled in the linen wrappings were a few small beads of blue faience.

Hall (C).

16. *An oval-shaped rush basket.* This basket is finely woven and measures 50 cms. across its long axis. It shows traces of coloured strands interwoven into the mesh at intervals to form triangular markings, but the colour of these markings has deteriorated. The lid has a flange round its lower edge to fit into a corresponding rim or flange on the inner side of the mouth of the basket itself (Pl. LXIV. 16).

Contents :—A pair of bronze forceps for extracting hair (Pl. LXV); note the curved ends made expressly for that purpose.

A razor very finely wrought of copper, with two separate cutting edges. One edge or blade is slightly concave for shaving the convex surfaces of the head, face, and body; the other blade is of convex shape for shaving the concave parts, such as the arm-pits (Pl. LXV). The preservation is so good that the knife edges are still keen, and the prints of the ancient finger-marks are still visible upon its polished surfaces. It measures 18.5 cms. in length.

A hone of granular white stone for sharpening the razor (Pl. LXV).

A kohl-box made of cedar-wood (?). It is octagonal in shape, and has an ivory lid and base. The lid turns on a stud-headed wooden peg, and when closed it was held in place by an ivory bolt shot into copper staples. On the side of the box, slung in two copper staples, is the ebony kohl-stick. The total length is 7.9 cms. (Pl. LXV).

The handle and clasp of a fan made of wood (Pl. LXV).

A pottery bowl (Pl. LXV).

An ebony kohl-stick.

A pair of leather sandals (these were adhering to the bottom of the basket, and could not be removed).

A large round basket (Pl. LXIV, right-hand side of illustration).

A small round basket (Pl. LXIV, left-hand side of illustration).

The large round basket contained :

A kohl-pot of hard grey stone like aragonite, and a kohl-stick of ebony (Pl. LXV).

A bronze mirror made of copper, measuring in its maximum length 17 cms. (Pl. LXV): the handle had been coated with a white metal (silver ?) to prevent corrosion.

A scarab made of green jasper and bearing the prenomen and nomen of Amenhetep I (Pls. LXV, LXXII. 16). It is round backed and a fine specimen.

Some decayed locks of hair.

The smaller round basket contained :

A blue glazed steatite scarab of the Hyksos Period (Pls. LXV, LXXII. 16).

17. *A chair and a stool.* These were broken and tucked between the foot of

Hall (C) (continued).

coffin No. 18 and the wall (Pl. LXXI). The chair made of wood has a low square seat of rush-work mesh plaited upon a frame and supported by four square legs; the legs are strengthened by cross-bars. The slanting, curved, compound back is dowelled into the frame of the seat, and it is stayed by uprights which are continuous from the back legs; it also had (now missing) a central strut at the back. These uprights and the central strut were fixed to the back of the chair by means of ivory pegs. The principal constructive joints of the main body of the chair are strengthened by angle-pieces of carved bent wood, and these angle-pieces when exposed to view are ornamented by being composed of several kinds of wood. The top rail of the back (missing) appears from some of the remaining ivory pegs to have been made of ivory. It measures 41 × 52 cms. square, the seat 28 cms. high, and the top rail of the back must have been something like 75 cms. when perfect. The stool had a similar seat to the chair, and it also has similar strengthening bars between the legs. It stands 16 cms. in height, and measures 38 × 35 cms. square.

18. *Decorated anthropoid coffin of the New Kingdom.* Ground colour white; head-dress and bands for hieroglyphs blue. The inscriptions, written in black, with linear hieroglyphs of the Intermediate Period style, do not give any name (Pl. LXII. 18).

Contents:—Mummy roughly wrapped. The sex was difficult to ascertain.

19. *Viscera box.* Small square box painted white and of inferior quality. The interior, divided into two compartments by a central partition, contained matter wrapped in linen like the viscera of a mummy.

20. *Viscera box.* Painted white, with the *de hetep seten* formula upon the lid giving the name ◯ 🦅 ⸮ 🦅 ⸮ Ta-nezem. Depicted upon the four sides of the box are human-headed canopic jars, with, written on either side, the usual formulae in vertical bands (Pl. LXI. 20). The interior, divided into four compartments, contained similar matter to No. 19 (see coffin No. 24).

21. *Plain rectangular flat-topped coffin.* Like No. 75 (broken).

Contents:—Mummy of a man covered with a sheet. At the side of the left shoulder a wooden head-rest (Pl. LXVIII. 21), with, engraved upon its stem, the deities *Bes* and *Taurt*. On the third finger of the left hand a scarab mounted on a silver ring (Pl. LXXII. 21). The scarab is round-backed, of green glazed steatite, and has inscribed upon its base the 'Divine Wife, Hatshepsût'.

22. *Plain rectangular flat-topped coffin.* Like No. 75 (broken).

Contents:—Mummy of a woman, decayed and fallen to pieces. In the débris traces of plaited hair and two red jasper scarabs (Pl. LXXII. 22).

74 THE LATE MIDDLE KINGDOM AND

Hall (C) (continued).

23. *Decorated anthropoid coffin of the New Empire.* Ground colour white. Head-dress, blue striated with yellow lines. Face, yellow, with the eye-sockets of bronze, eyeballs of aragonite, and pupils of obsidian. Decoration, round the neck a collarette painted to represent rows of coloured beads, fringed with drop pendants, and with hawk-headed clasps. Below, over the breast, the vulture *Nekhebyt* and goddess *Nut*. On either side, at the ankles, the jackal *Anubis* is represented resting on his pylon. At the feet *Isis* and at the head *Nephthys*. There are three transverse bands round the body and one longitudinal band down the front, all of which contain the usual religious formulae with the owner's name ☥ Tahuti. On the sides of the shell, in the panels formed by the bands of hieroglyphs, are representations of the different gods facing legends dedicated to them. The lid was fixed to its shell by stud-headed wooden pegs.

Contents:—Mummy of a man with his hands crossed over the thighs. On the third finger of the left hand, attached by string, was a round-backed green glazed steatite scarab (Pl. LXXII. 23).

Beneath the coffin, and lying on the floor of the chamber, was a walking staff 142 cms. in length. The bark upon the stick was intact and it resembles that of cherry wood. The end was worn, and at the handle a natural projecting branch was trimmed so as to form a crutch.

24. *Decorated anthropoid coffin of the New Empire.* This coffin was similar to No. 23, but not so fine. The eyes were only painted, and the decoration varied by having the goddess *Nut* alone below the collar, the absence of the two jackals on the sides of the ankles, and *Nephthys* on the head. The legends, between the bands of formulae, referring to the gods had been added in black ink after the completion of the coffin. It bore the name ☥ Aah-hetep, who was called ☥ Ta-nezem (see viscera box No. 20).

Contents:—Mummy of a woman carefully wrapped, with the right arm across the breast, and the left arm resting at the side. She was covered with a sheet which when removed exposed two statuettes lying on either side of the knees of the mummy (Pl. LXVII. 2), and upon the shins a round shallow basket (Pl. LXIV. 24) containing a heart scarab made of unburnt steatite bearing an enigmatical inscription (Pl. LXXII. 24). On the left hand, tied with string to the third finger, were two scarabs: one, high-backed and of blue glazed steatite, bore the name of the 'Herald Ren-senb'; the other, high-backed and of blue paste, had a winged *kheper* surmounted by *Ra* engraved upon its base (Pl. LXXII. 24). Underneath the mummy was a very small basket containing three copper forceps and a kohl-stick.

INTERMEDIATE PERIOD NECROPOLIS

Hall (C) (continued).

The statuette found on the right side may be described as follows: Small portrait figure of a boy named ☐☐☐ Amenemheb, nude, and of electrum; dedicated by his father Tahuti[1] 'who makes to live his name'. It measures 18 cms. high, and stands upon a wooden pedestal which is inscribed. The work is that of a very good artist, showing great instinctive feeling and subtle modelling as well as delicacy. Though the actual finish of the detail is not carried to a very high pitch, this fact does not lessen its beauty, and a glance at the photographs (Pl. LXVII. 1 and frontispiece) will at once show its charm and high art sense. In the left hand is a lotus-bud with long and flowing stalk. The metal was cast and the figure worked upon after it was chilled. The statuette at first may seem attenuated, but any one who knows the youth of modern Egypt will at once recognize its truth.

The statuette found on the left side was in wood, of a boy named ☐☐☐ Hu-uben-ef, and it was dedicated by his father Tahuti 'who makes to live his name'. This figure stands 31 cms. in height, and is very cleanly cut, the work good, but of a different and perhaps not so high a standard as the metal figure of his brother. Nevertheless it is exquisitely rendered and shows a strong likeness to the other, particularly in the shape of the head. The pedestal is inscribed with the dedication, and mentions also a prayer for *per-kheru* offerings for the *ka*. Traces of colour, red, are visible on the nude parts; the hair is coloured black, the eye-balls are painted white, the pupils, eye-lashes, and brows black (Pl. LXVII. 2).

25. *An oval-shaped basket*. This basket is similar in make to No. 16 and measures 40 cms. across its long axis. It is of coarser weaving and shows no signs of decorations (Pl. LXIV. 25). Some bituminous material had been spilt into it, and many of the objects it contained adhered to its inner side and were stuck together from that cause.

Contents (Pl. LXVI):—It seemed to have contained a scribe's outfit, which was once probably complete, but many of the objects found in it were broken and parts of them were missing. These were: (1) a large reed case made of a section cut from the stalk of a thick rush. At the top this has a floral ornament made of four pieces of carved wood which are let into spaces cut in the sides at the end and bound in position by a strip of linen. The node or natural joint of the rush has been utilized for the bottom end, and the top end was stopped by a rag plug. In it were

---

[1] See coffin No. 23.

Hall (C) (continued).

found twenty-six thin reeds and a few seeds of a plant.[1] (2) A small reed case made like the former one described above, but without top ornament. It enclosed fifteen thin reeds and similar seeds of a plant.[1] (3) A wooden palette varying only from the common and well-known types by having three small oblong-shaped holes pierced diagonally through the side corners for strips of leather (?) for suspension. (4) A peculiar wooden instrument, mallet-like in shape: its use is unknown to me. There are on the small end indentations like marks that could be caused by tightly-bound string. (5) A rectangular oblong piece of hard wood. Its use is unknown to me; but it appears to be part of some instrument, as there are two holes in one side and another at the end. In all three holes there are ends of broken pegs. (6) A stick some 80 cms. in length. It seems to be the cross-bar of a pair of scales (note the hole and peg in the centre and peculiar notched ends). (7) A bag made of woven fibrous string. (8) A small linen bag; the mouth was drawn together by string in the same manner as purses of the present day. (9) A roll of leather, bound with strips of the same material. (10) A roll of linen (not shown in the Plate). (11) Very small fragments of papyrus which seem to have been torn from a small roll of papyrus (not shown in the Plate). (12) A clay figure of a cynocephalous ape (Thoth). This little creature was wrapped in linen. (13) Human-headed sphinx, cut out of a sheet of copper. (14) A large round piece of wax. (15) A tortoise-shell. (16) A miniature clay cup. A strip of linen was bound round the stem. (17) Model knuckle-bone in clay. (18) Some pieces of resinous material. (19) A small wooden peg. (20) A small amuletic figure in green glaze faience. (21) One large clay disk, four wax disks, and twelve disks of different sizes made of some black material. They appear to be weights:

1.	Clay	12·0 grains.
2.	Wax	4·0 ,,
3.	,,	4·0 ,,
4.	,,	— ⎫ weight obscured from bitumen
5.	,,	— ⎭ adhering to them.
6.	Black material	3·5 grains.
7.	,, ,,	3·5 ,,
8.	,, ,,	3·5 ,,
9.	,, ,,	3·0 ,,
10.	,, ,,	— broken.
11.	,, ,,	3·0 grains.

---

[1] These seeds, too far gone to be recognized, are shown in Pl. LXVI, above the figure of the ape.

Hall (C) (continued).

  12. Black material 2·5 grains.
  13. ,, ,, 2·5 ,,
  14. ,, ,, 2·5 ,,
  15. ,, ,, 2·5 ,,
  16. ,, ,, 2·5 ,,
  17. ,, ,, 2·0 ,,

26. *A writing tablet.* This tablet, made of wood and covered with stucco, with surface polished for writing, bore inscriptions on both sides. It was broken in two halves, measures 48 × 26·5 cms., and was found among the stones covering the floor of the chamber (see Chapter XIII by Dr. Möller).

27. *Parts of a model five-stringed musical instrument.* Similar to Nos. 28, 63 A, and 92 (see Pl. LXXI, and for description No. 63 A).

28. *A pottery pan containing various objects.* (1) A model four-stringed musical instrument (Pl. LXXI. 28) made of sycamore wood, ebony, and ivory. (For further description see No. 63 A.) (2) A bird-trap (Pl. LXIV. 28) made of wood and of the following construction and mechanism:— Two flat boards cut semicircular and joined in the middle by a central broad bar of wood which is slightly longer than the diameter of the circle formed by the two semicircular boards; these three pieces of wood formed the floor of the trap. Upon the central bar, it will be noticed that there are two pairs of pillars, grooved on top, and a hole in the bar on the right and left side of each pair of pillars (see Pl. LXIV). Strung over each pair of pillars were (now missing) several strands of catgut (?), with their ends passed through the holes on either side, and held at the back by short pieces of stick. By revolving these pieces of stick at the back the strands of catgut were twisted and brought to any degree of tension required, and thus by this method formed two spring-hinges. Fixed in these spring-hinges was a flexible piece of stick bent to form an arched bow (not shown in Pl. LXIV), either end of the bow being passed through the strands of twisted gut at such an angle as to cause the bow to be pressed on to one half of the circular bottom of the trap (the position when closed). Attached to the bow and on the opposite half of the bottom of the trap was a net (see holes for this purpose and remains of net, Pl. LXIV. 28), sufficiently large to allow the capture of a bird. To open the trap, the bow would be pulled over to the side that the net is attached to. On this side, at the edge, there is a notch (see Pl. LXIV. 28) for a pillar-catch which held the bow open. This catch was worked by a string through a hole beside it (see Pl. LXIV. 28), which was passed underneath and brought up through a hole in the centre of the bottom of the trap (see Pl. LXIV. 28),

Hall (C) (continued).

where the string was attached to a sensitive adjustment so placed that the movements of a bird touching it would detach it and cause the trap to close (i. e. the bow to spring into its original position on the opposite side). The wooden bow belonging to the trap was found sometime afterwards among a lot of stray wood that came from the tomb, and it was exactly as described above. (3) A mechanical toy bird made of wood (Pl. LXIV, right and left of trap). (4) Pottery bowl of red pottery full of a brown powdery substance. (5) A painted clay head of a bull. (6) A small round basket containing a blue faience kohl-pot. (7) A writing tablet like No. 26 (see Chapter XIII by Dr. Möller).

29. *Plain anthropoid coffin.* The outer surface of this coffin is painted white, with the features of the face roughly delineated in black (Pl. LXI. 29).
    Contents:—Mummy of a girl.
30. *Rectangular child's coffin.* Similar to No. 80.
    Contents:—Skeleton of a baby.
31. *Dug-out rectangular child's coffin.* Similar to No. 41.
    Contents:—Mummy of a child. In the wrappings covering the hair were some bone and cornelian beads like those found in coffin No. 78 given in Pl. LXXII. 78. Resting on the feet of the mummy was a basket turned over and its contents spilt. The contents were several necklaces of many kinds of blue faience beads, of which examples are given in Pl. LXXIII. 81. With them was a small blue faience kohl-pot of usual type. One of the cowroid beads bore the prenomen of Thothmes I, while others had hieroglyphic signs on them, including one which had upon its base.
32. *A bunch of papyrus reeds.*
33. *A small obsidian unguent vase.* This was found resting upon the chest of coffin No. 28.
34. *Plain rectangular flat-topped coffin.* Similar to No. 75 (broken).
    Contents:—Mummy broken to fragments.
35. *Decorated rectangular coffin.* Smashed to pieces by the falling of the rock ceiling of the chamber. There were no traces of objects.
36. *Plain rectangular flat-topped coffin.* Similar to No. 75.
    Contents:—Among the decayed remains of a mummy was a round-backed green glazed steatite scarab, bearing a very fine example of spiral pattern engraved upon its bezel (Pl. LXXII. 36).
37. *Rectangular dug-out coffin.* Similar to No. 58 (lid missing).
    Contents:—Mummy of a woman. In the débris of the mummy, on the bottom of the coffin, was a round-backed green glazed steatite scarab (Pl. LXXII. 37).

INTERMEDIATE PERIOD NECROPOLIS

Hall (C) (continued).

38. *Plain anthropoid coffin.* Similar to No. 29.
    Contents:—Mummy of a man. Lying on the bottom of the coffin was a blue faience scaraboid bead (Pl. LXXII. 38).
39. *Parts of a frame of a wooden stool.* Similar to No. 18.
40. *Anthropoid dug-out child's coffin.* Painted white and very roughly made.
    Contents:—Child's skeleton.

Pit (D).

41. *Rectangular dug-out child's coffin.* The shell was cut out of one block of wood, and for the lid a flat board was used. Wooden pegs at either end of the lid show that it once had head and foot pieces (Pl. LXI. 41).
    Contents:—Mummy of a child.
42. *Rectangular dug-out child's coffin.* This was of peculiar type. The block of wood from which it was made was cut in half diagonally, so that the lid and shell were of equal proportions. Some auxiliary pieces of wood had been let into the lid to strengthen it (Pl. LXI. 42).
    Contents:—Skeleton of a baby.
43. *Rectangular child's coffin.* Similar to No. 80.
    Contents:—Skeleton of a very young child. In the shell of the coffin there were a few miniature blue faience beads.
44. *Rectangular child's coffin.* Similar to No. 80. The lid was tied on with rope.
    Contents:—Skeleton of a child.
45. *Rectangular child's coffin.* Similar to No. 80.
    Contents:—Mummy of a child.
46. *Plain rectangular flat-topped coffin.* Similar to No. 75.
    Contents:—Mummy of a man.
47. *Plain anthropoid coffin.* Similar to No. 29. The lid was tied on with rope.
    Contents:—Mummy of a woman, in bad condition and much decayed. In the débris there were some bone bead-bangles (for example see Pl. LXXIII. 53); a blue glazed steatite scarab of the Hyksos period; a turquoise blue glass cowroid bead; and a blue faience scaraboid bead (Pl. LXXII. 47).
48. *Plain rectangular flat-topped coffin.* Similar to No. 75.
    Contents:—Mummy of a man.
49. *Plain rectangular flat-topped coffin.* Similar to No. 75.
    Contents:—Two mummies; one of a man, the other of a woman, lying head to feet. Among these remains were some bone and cornelian bead-bangles (for example see Pl. LXXIII. 78).
50. *Rectangular open-grid bottomed coffin.* Similar to No. 52.
    Contents:—Mummy of a half-grown child. The mummy was enveloped in reeds. Upon it were bone and cornelian bead-bangles (see Pl. LXXIII. 78); a group of tubular barrel-shaped beads, coated

Pit (D) (continued).

with chips of glass and disk-shaped faience beads; also an amuletic necklace (Pl. LXXIII. 50). The beads of this amuletic necklace were made of cornelian, faience, and blue opaque glass; the amulets were flies, hawks, and symbolical knots, made of glazed and unglazed steatite, jasper, and faience, and the central pendant of gold. The original position of these objects upon the mummy it was impossible to ascertain.

51. *Rectangular dug-out child's coffin.* Similar to No. 41.

Contents:—Mummy of a child. In the coffin, underneath the mummy, was a wooden throw-stick and a gold earring; the second gold earring was afterwards found at the bottom of the pit. The throw-stick, 42 cms. in length, is finely carved out of very hard wood, and it has a propeller-like twist.

52. *Rectangular open-grid bottomed coffin.* A plain wood rectangular coffin, with wooden bars at intervals in place of the boarded bottom (Pl. LX. 52).

Contents:—Mummy of a woman, bent, as it was too large for the coffin. On the third finger of the left hand, attached by string, were two jasper scarabs (Pl. LXXII. 52). One of the scarabs had a fish and lotus-flower engraved upon its bezel.

53. *Plain rectangular gable-topped coffin.* Similar to No. 62, but has no traces of paint.

Contents:—Mummy of a man. Beside the head, and resting on the bottom of the coffin, were:—(1) a small wood and ivory jewel-box (fallen to pieces); (2) an alabaster bowl in the shape of a cartouche; (3) a blue faience bowl; and (4) a pottery vase (Pl. LXIX. 53). The mummy had rotted away, and among the débris were:—(1) round-backed blue glazed steatite scarab, mounted in a gold funda, bearing on its base the name of the royal daughter, Neferu-ra (daughter of Queen Hatshepsût); (2) round-backed blue glazed scarab bearing the prenomen of Thothmes III; (3) round-backed green glazed scarab, mounted in gold funda, bearing a decorative pattern; (4) cowroid seal of glazed steatite (worn to brown) bearing a decorative pattern, and mounted in a gold funda; (5) high-backed scarab of dark green paste bearing a floral pattern, and mounted upon a copper-wire ring—the wire is threaded through the scarab and is passed through a small hole on the other end of the wire, flattened and pierced for the purpose, and it is held thus by being twisted round the wire a few times (Pl. LXXII. 53). Fallen out of the small jewel-box (mentioned above) there were three necklaces. One of them was a long string of violet faience beads (similar to No. 6, Pl. LXXIII); another was made up of plain bone beads (Pl. LXXIII. 53); and the third consisted of cornelian, violet faience, and gold beads, with amulets at intervals made of gold, silver, cornelian, and blue glass (Pl. LXXIII. 53).

INTERMEDIATE PERIOD NECROPOLIS

Pit (D) (continued).

54. *A grey pottery vase* (Pl. LXXIV. D), bearing a hieratic inscription (see Chapter XIII, by Dr. Möller).

55. *Plain rectangular flat-topped coffin.* Similar to No. 75.

Contents:—Two adult and one child's mummy. Like the coffin they were very much broken. Among the remains were bone and cornelian beads, and an ivory bracelet (Pl. LXXIII. 55, on the plate incorrectly 85).

56. *Rectangular child's coffin.* Similar to No. 80.

Contents:—Mummy of an infant.

57. *Plain rectangular flat-topped coffin.* Similar to No. 75.

Contents:—Three adult mummies, which, like the coffin, were broken. With them was a wooden head-rest (Pl. LXVIII. 57); a round-backed green glazed steatite scarab (Pl. LXXII. 57); and a few stray beads of cornelian, faience, and bone.

58. *Rectangular dug-out coffin.* The lid was tied on with rope (Pl. LXI. 58).

Contents:—Mummy of a man.

59. *Decorated rectangular coffin.* The colouring is similar to that of No. 7, except that instead of the two goddesses at either end there are geometrical drawings (Pl. LX. 59).

Contents:—Four mummies covered with a large shroud. At the head end of the coffin, and resting on the mummies, there were: (1) a black pottery vase; (2) a red pottery biangular bowl; (3) a wooden head-rest; (4) a basket containing four dôm nuts, and a vase which had in it a piece of crystal, and a round-backed green glazed steatite scarab (Pl. LXVIII. 59 and Pl. LXXII. 59).

The four mummies, packed head to feet, were as follows:—

(a) Mummy of a woman with a scarab necklace (Pl. LXXII. 59 A); a bead necklace (Pl. LXXIII. 59); and some bead-bangles of bone and cornelian (for examples see No. 78, Pl. LXXIII). One of the scarabs upon the necklace bears the nomen of Thothmes I.

(b) Mummy of a child.

(c) Mummy of a man wrapped in very coarse linen.

(d) Mummy of an adult (sex difficult to ascertain).

With the mummy there was a walking-staff; in the abdomen were some dôm nuts, and a group of scarabs (Pl. LXXII. 59 D), which appear, from the string that some were still threaded upon, to have once formed a necklace. In the wrappings near the neck of the mummy were some faience and bone beads. One of the scarabs bore upon its bezel ○ ⌇ Neb-ded-Ra, encircled by a coil pattern (cp. Scarab, B.M., No. 87780); another had the prenomen of Thothmes II, above a crouching jackal; and a third one has the *Hor-nub* name of Thothmes I.

Chamber (E).

60. *Rishi coffin.* Similar to No. 11, but of very rough workmanship.

    Contents:—Mummy of a woman scantily wrapped in coarse linen.

61. *Rectangular child's coffin.* Similar to No. 80.

    Contents:—Mummy of an infant.

62. *Plain rectangular gable-topped coffin.* The outer surface of this coffin is covered with a thin paint of pinky hue. The lid is slanting on either side, has a longitudinal beam in the centre, and an upright head and foot piece on its ends (Pl. LX. 62).

    Contents:—Three mummies: two were of adults lying side by side, the third of a child placed at their feet. The child's mummy had upon its neck an amuletic necklace composed of round and barrel faience beads of red and green colour with pendant amulets of the same material, and in the centre a brown stone turtle; on the arms were bead-bangles composed of bone and faience beads; and lying near the hands, tied upon a piece of string, were two scarabs and a cowroid seal (Pl. LXXII. 62 A). One of the adult mummies had round its neck a cornelian bead necklace (Pl. LXXIII. 62); and upon the third finger of the left hand a green glazed steatite scarab (Pl. LXXII. 62 B).

63. *Decorated rectangular coffin.* The coloration of the detail, painted upon a strawberry-coloured ground, is similar to No. 7. On the end panels, the goddesses *Isis* and *Nephthys* are standing with the arms upheld (Pl. LX. 63).

    Contents:—Two mummies of a man and a woman, lying side by side, and covered with a shroud. Beside the head of the woman were two grey pottery vases, and a larger one in black pottery; a dark blue faience bowl, and a wooden kohl-pot (Pl. LXVIII. 63). The woman had within the wrappings of the head a broken ivory comb (Pl. LXVIII. 63); and near the hands, lying loosely, were two cowroid seals (Pl. LXXII. 63 A). The man had no ornament upon him.

63 A. *A four-stringed musical instrument* (Pl. LXXI. 63 A). The *neck*, *back*, and *belly* are made of one piece of sycamore wood. The *belly* is hollowed out like a trough, and has its two sides curved slightly inwards at the middle, thus forming a kind of waist (this was probably due to the tension of the strained skin that covered it). Across the *belly*, longitudinally, is the combined *tail-piece* and *bridge* to which the lower fixed ends of the strings are attached: the tapering end of this combined *tail-piece* and *bridge* was inserted into a socket at the juncture where the *belly* and *neck* join, and its lower and broader end was bound to a protuberance, made for the purpose, at the extreme end of the *belly*. Near the top end of the *neck*, and into the back of it, the four *key-pegs* for receiving the strings are inserted. The strings themselves (their lower ends being fixed to the combined *tail-piece* and *bridge*),

Chamber (E) (continued).

which were passed along the side of the *neck* and twisted round the *key-pegs*, had their upper ends brought over the *neck* and slipped under the tightened portion of the strings which pressed against the side of the *neck* (see Fig. 92, Pl. LXXI). For a *sounding-board*, skin was stretched over the whole of the *belly*, with an aperture left at the juncture of the *belly* and *neck* to allow the combined *tail-piece* and *bridge* to be inserted into its socket. The total length of the instrument is 1·37 metres. This particular specimen I believe to have been an actual instrument, while the others, Nos. 27, 28, and 92, were merely small models. With these models there are slight variations in the construction, but as the main idea is the same it is unnecessary to describe them.

64. *Plain rectangular gable-topped coffin.* Similar to No. 62, but has no traces of colour upon it.

Contents:—Mummy of a man sewn up in a shroud. Near the head a wooden head-rest; by the side a walking-staff; and under the head, wrapped in a piece of linen, were (1) a wooden kohl-pot of trefoil section, (2) a bronze razor and granular stone hone,[1] (3) a cord belt and loin cloth (Pl. LXIX. 64). On the third finger of the left hand was a blue glazed steatite scarab, mounted on gold funda: this was tied with string (Pl. LXXII. 64).

65. *Plain rectangular gable-topped coffin.* Similar to No. 62, but with no traces of colour.

Contents:—Two mummies of a man and woman, lying head to feet, and covered by a shroud. The mummy of the woman had a broken alabaster bowl (Pl. LXIX. 65) lying at the feet. The mummy of the man appeared to be re-wrapped, and had nothing on it.

66. *Rishi coffin.* Shell—cut out of a tree trunk, and painted with black, red, and white bands. Lid—the detailed feather-decoration is painted in red, green, and dark blue on a white and yellow ground. The face is yellow. The longitudinal band down the centre has no inscription (Pl. LXII. 66).

Contents:—Mummy of a man.

67. *Rectangular child's coffin.* This coffin had been enlarged, and the lid, which was made of old boards, was tied to pegs at either end of the shell.

Contents:—Mummy of a child, with knees bent.

Chamber (A).

68. *Semi-decorated anthropoid coffin.* Similar to No. 6 (Pl. LVIII. 68).

Contents:—A skeleton of a young man with hardly any traces of mummification visible.

[1] See No. 16.

Chamber (A) (continued).

69. *Plain rectangular gable-topped coffin.* Similar to No. 62 (Pl. LVIII. 69).

    Contents:—Mummy of a woman much decayed.

70. *Rishi coffin.* Similar to No. 66. The longitudinal band down the front has the *de hetep seten* formula, but bears no name: space for the name has been left blank (Pl. LVIII. 70).

    Contents:—Mummy of a woman lying flat on her back, with head turned towards the left. In front of the face, a wooden head-rest; under the cheek, a large bronze mirror. On the head was a wig of plaited hair (Pl. LXX. 70).

71. *Plain rectangular gable-topped coffin.* Similar to No. 62. The bottom of the coffin was not in place, and was lying on the floor, only partly under it.

    Contents:—Mummy of a woman covered with a mat with long pile. On her right side, a wooden cylinder covered with leather and containing six musical reeds. These reeds were (1) 36·5 cms. long, with four notes; (2) 36·5 cms. long, with three notes; (3) 30·5 cms. long, with two notes; (4) 28 cms. long, with four notes on one side (three were intentionally blocked up with resinous material), and on the other side there was a hole or note; (5) 25 cms. long, with five notes (a crack mended with resinous material); (6) 23·5 cms. long, with five notes. The reeds average 12 mms. in thickness. Under the woman's legs was a basket containing two flints, two lumps of clay, a reed kohl-pot and two wooden kohl-sticks, a piece of a wooden comb,[1] a splinter of wood, some bone and faience bead-bangles, and a small plaited lock of hair. In the womb were traces of an embryonic skeleton (Pl. LXIX. 71).

72. *Viscera box.* Similar to No. 20, with rounded lid (Pl. LXI. 72). No inscriptions.

    Contents like Nos. 19 and 20.

73. *Decorated anthropoid coffin of the New Empire.* Similar in fashion to No. 28, but rougher in detail and finish (Pls. LVIII and LXII. 73). The lid was fixed in place by wooden pegs, and it bore the name Aahmes.

    Contents:—Mummy of a woman covered with a shroud. On the right side of the head was a broken kohl-pot; and at the top of the head, rolled in linen, a chignon, a pottery vase containing a kind of pomade which bore prints of the ancient fingers, and an ebony comb and bone hair-pin (Pl. LXX. 73). The mummy was sewn up in a sheet, which, when removed, exposed transverse bindings which continued down to the bitumenized body. The arms were crossed over the abdomen. On the head, over the natural hair, a plaited wig much decayed.

---

[1] See 73.

Chamber (A) (continued).

74. *Decorated anthropoid coffin of the New Empire.* This coffin (Pl. LVIII. 74) is fully illustrated by Plate LXIII, Figs. 1, 2. It bears the name of [hieroglyphs] Mentu-hetep, and, among the religious formulae written upon it, gives the variant [hieroglyph] for *Horus*.

   Contents :—Mummy of a man covered with a shroud. Under the shroud, and resting upon the mummy, was a long (164 cms.) bronze snake sceptre; and on the third finger of the left hand a round-backed green glazed steatite scarab (Pl. LXXII. 74) tied with string.

75. *Plain rectangular flat-topped coffin.* Lid and shell made of planks of wood, with upright head and foot pieces upon the ends of lid (Pls. LVIII, LX. 75).

   Contents :—Mummy of a woman with plaited hair. Round the waist was a girdle composed of two twisted strings of bone beads.

76. *Plain rectangular flat-topped coffin.* Similar to No. 75.

   Contents :—Mummy of a woman. Hair plaited; on wrists, bangles of double strings of bone and cornelian beads; on third finger of left hand a scarab (Pl. LXXII. 76), and few beads strung on thread; and tied round the fourth finger of the same hand was a small cornelian pendant drop.

Chamber (B).

77. *Plain rectangular gable-topped coffin* (Pl. LIX. 77). Similar to No. 62.

   Contents :—Three mummies covered with a shroud: one was of a man, and the other two of children. The children's mummies were bitumenized and bound in knotted and twisted linen. The mummy of the man (bearded) had on the third finger of the left hand a scarab mounted upon a silver ring (Pl. LXXII. 77 C). The scarab, made of steatite (brown), bore an ornamental Hathor design.

78. *Plain rectangular flat-topped coffin* (Pl. LIX. 78). Similar to No. 75.

   Contents :—Mummy of a woman covered with a shroud. Under the head a basket containing a dark brown stone kohl-pot, an alabaster vase, and a cedar-wood comb. Near the basket were two black pottery long-necked vases (Pl. LXVIII. 78). Lying on the breast, and under the wrappings, was a small basket (Pl. LXVIII. 78) containing bone and cornelian bead-bangles (Pl. LXXIII. 78), and three scarabs and two cowroids. On the neck an amuletic necklace; and on the third finger of the left hand two gold-mounted cowroids. The scarabs were two of glazed steatite mounted in gold fundi, and one of cornelian; the cowroids were three of glass mounted in gold, and one of steatite mounted in gold (Pl. LXXII. 78). The amuletic necklace was composed of lapis-lazuli, gold, cornelian, and garnet beads, strung more or less haphazard between gold amulets (Pl. LXXIII. 78).

Chamber (B) (continued).

79. *Plain rectangular flat-topped coffin* (Pl. LIX. 79). Similar to No. 75 (head and foot pieces missing and lid partly open).

  Contents:—Mummy of a young woman, which appeared to have been re-wrapped. On the neck a necklace (Pl. LXXIII. 79) composed of gold, lapis-lazuli, and cornelian beads.

80. *Rectangular child's coffin.* Square box, oblong in form, made of wooden planks. The lid had upright head and foot pieces (Pls. LIX and LXI. 80).

  Contents:—Mummy of an infant.

South Wing.

81. *Plain rectangular flat-topped coffin.* Similar to No. 75. This coffin was open, its lid lying by its side, and was empty.

North Wing.

82. *Two ivory castanets.* The ends shaped like human hands, and curved. They were lying in the débris of the corridor of the tomb.

Niche (G).

83. *Plain rectangular gable-topped coffin.* Similar to No. 62, but of small size and thinly coated with white paint. Upon the top of the coffin was a decayed mummy of a person of immature age, and with it were three gold earrings (Pl. LXIX. 83). The contents of the coffin were two children's mummies lying one upon the other, and resting upon the top one was a small round basket (Pl. LXIX. 83) containing: (1) a wristlet of bone and cornelian beads (Pl. LXXIII. 83); (2) a necklace of bone beads (for example see 53, Pl. LXXIII); and (3) a necklace of violet faience beads. Upon the lower mummy were two small bundles of linen containing fruit of the *nebek*-tree, which were bound together with a string of blue faience beads. This mummy had upon its left wrist (?) a bangle of bone and faience beads (Pl. LXXIII. 83).

  Behind the coffin were three pots (Pl. LXXIV. G) leaning against the back wall of the niche. The niche (G) seems to have been specially made for these burials, which were covered up by the stone chippings made in its excavation. These burials appear to have been made in the tomb when left open after its destruction, but before it was used as a storehouse.

Passage (L).

84. *Dug-out anthropoid child's coffin.* The shell, cut out of a tree stem, was very roughly made. The lid was missing.

  Contents:—Mummy of an infant decayed, and among the débris were minute blue faience and gold beads (Pl. LXXIII. 84).

Central Passage.

85. *An ivory castanet.* Burnt, and with end shaped like a human hand; it differed from No. 82 by being straight. This was found in the layer of rubbish that covered the floor of the passage. It appears to belong to the original interment of the tomb.

Hall (C).

86. *A wooden statuette and fragment of a wooden coffin of the Middle Kingdom.* The statuette, broken, is covered with stucco and painted, and is of exceedingly coarse workmanship. It represents a woman carrying upon her head a linen basket. The fragment of coffin bore an inscription reading [hieroglyphs] *perkheru*-offerings for the devoted one *Henyt*. These antiquities were found in the layer of rubbish that covered the floor, and probably belong to the original interment of the tomb (some parts of the statuette came from the small chamber *F*).

87. *A wooden jewel-box.* This is similar to the box found in tomb No. 24 (Pl. XLVI).

   Contents:—A *ka-hetep* amulet and necklace of blue faience (Pl. LXXIII. 87); a necklace of white and violet cylindrical faience beads (Pl. LXXIII. 87); a blue glazed steatite scarab (Pl. LXXII. 87); a blue glazed steatite kohl-pot, made to imitate matrix of turquoise; a reel of white faience; and a copper fillet for the hair (see tomb No. 25, p. 55). These objects are all of the Middle Kingdom period, and were discovered in the layer of rubbish covering the floor of the chamber. They probably belonged to the original interment.

Pit (D).

88. *Panel stela.* Covered with white stucco and painted. It measures 45 × 27 cms. (see Chapter XIII, by Dr. Möller).
89. *Panel stela.* Similar to No. 88, and measures 57 × 22 cms. (see Chapter XIII, by Dr. Möller).
90. *Panel stela.* Similar to Nos. 88 and 89, but of much thicker wood, and badly broken (see Chapter XIII, by Dr. Möller).

Chamber (F).

91. *Broken shafts of arrows, parts of bows, a wooden mallet, and a wooden hoe.* These antiquities came from the rubbish in chamber *F*, at the bottom of pit *D*.
92. *Parts of a four-stringed musical instrument.* See No. 63 A, also Pl. LXXI. 92.

Pottery. Examples of the different kinds of pottery vessels found in this tomb are figured in Pl. LXXIV.

The letters and figures refer to the lettering on the Plan (Pl. LV). The four specimens marked GEN. came from the corridor and passage.

In the right corner of the plate are examples of mud-sealings found in the rubbish that covered the floor.

Pit Tombs Nos. 38 and 39.

Both these are of common pit-tomb type, and were possibly made for the retainers of the owner of tomb No. 37. They were carefully examined but found to be plundered. Only a few fragments of pottery vessels similar to those from tombs No. 24 and 25 were found in the sand filling them (Pl. XXX).

Tomb No. 41.

A large tomb south of No. 37. This has not yet been excavated or examined, for it was only discovered a few days before ending the work of season 1911 (Pl. XXX).

CHAPTER XIII

THE HIERATIC TEXTS OF TOMB NO. 37

By George Möller

89. *Wooden stela of Ihŷ* (Pl. LXXV). This tablet is composed of two boards held together by pegs or dowels, and covered with a fine coat of stucco, the surface of which has been polished to receive the writing. Upon it are the following representations:—Above, to the right, is drawn the sacred Barque of Sokaris; below, to the left, is figured the deceased with staff and sceptre, and before him, a boy offering a goose, a table with offerings, a lotus-flower, loaves of bread, joints of meat, &c. The legend is in the hieratic writing typical of the Hyksos period, and reads:—

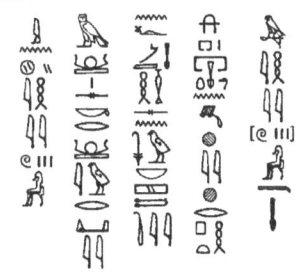

'Ihŷ comes in the boat of Sokaris; to him has been granted justification.[1] He is favoured of the Lord of the Shrine.[2] A *perkheru*-offering in bread and wild fowl to the veteran in the presence of Ptah, Ihŷ, justified.'

Below the figure of deceased is:—

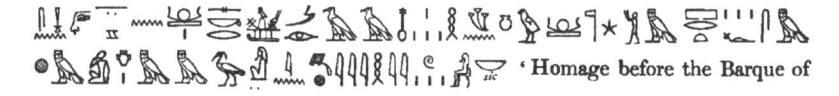

'Homage before the Barque of

---

[1] The justified dead. [2] i.e. the god Sokaris.

90 THE HIERATIC TEXTS OF TOMB NO. 37

Sokaris, viewing the beauties of the Holy Ship, adoring at his coming forth, joyous among the glorified Spirits, the veteran Ihŷ, Lord (of Worthiness).'

Below the figure is [hieroglyphs] 'The Veteran Ihŷ, justified.'

90. Wooden stela of an unknown lady (Pl. LXXVI. 8). The stucco has mostly peeled off, and only the representation of the offerings (on right side) are well preserved. The figure of the deceased is almost entirely destroyed, and only the beginning of the inscription is preserved: [hieroglyphs] 'M ...... comes ......'

88. Wooden stela of the [hieroglyphs] (Pl. LXXV), 'One held worthy by Ptah-Sokar, the Lord of the Shrine,'[1] the Steward ...... y, justified.' In the legend the name of the deceased is destroyed, and the title 'steward' is partly broken. The figure shows the deceased standing with a staff in his left hand.

54. Pot of burnt clay (Pl. LXXIV. D) with two lines of hieratic text giving the beginning of a rough draft for a letter:—

[hieroglyphs]

[hieroglyphs]

'Harmose to Ahhotep, Life, Wealth, Health, and the Favour of Amon-Re! Behold, I have not found ... I have permitted that something be brought to me.'

The break in the middle of the second line makes the meaning of the text impossible to interpret.

Regarding the date, it is to be noted that the script is typical of the late Hyksos period, or of the beginning of the XVIIIth Dynasty, and may be compared with that of the Papyrus Ebers.

26. Writing tablet of wood covered with stucco (Pls. LXXVII, LXXVIII). The text on the obverse contains a letter, perhaps not an original document, but an exercise. This supposition is borne out by the fact that the text on the reverse of the tablet is written in a clumsy handwriting.

The beginning of the text can be restored by the help of an ostracon in the Berlin Museum (P. 12866); the lacunae at the beginning of lines 8-10 are, however, wanting. The text is, moreover, very faulty, so that the following translation, in which I was fortunate enough to have Prof. Erman's help, is only given with reservations:—

---

[1] The god of the dead of Memphis (Saqqarah).

'(1) The servant speaks to his lord, [from whom he desires to receive life, prosperity, and health] throughout the length (2) of eternity, for ever, just as [this servant[1] desires. Mayest thou be justi]fied before (3) the Spirits[2] of Heliopolis and before the gods. [*May they grant thee*] all good [*things*] every day, (4) as I desire it, so that [*all*] thy affairs [*under the protection*] of Month, (5) the Lord of Thebes, may be as I desire; may Ptah, Lord of Memphis, rejoice his heart (that of the person addressed) with a very good life, (6) as well as a good old age, and that he may attain to a state of worthiness, so that his worthiness may come before Month, (7) Lord of Thebes, as I desire it, in peace, and great comfort. But this letter [(8) *which thou hast written me, as far as that is concerned, give thyself*] with regard to it, [*no anxiety*]. I shall be of thy mind. Mayest thou

[1] The familiar alternative for 'I'. [In the following it can therefore be translated by 'I'.

[2] That is to say, 'gods.'

92 THE HIERATIC TEXTS OF TOMB NO. 87

be gracious towards (?) NBT ... (9) .... this ......, causing to send out ... (10) ...... with myrrh of Punt and pleasing odours of God's Land,[1] (11) clothed in the *d3jw*-garment, which (?) I make. The poor man, he sees (12) .... thou seest thy wife there ill[2] as she weeps (13) over thee. She weeps over thee. Thy fish of the night, thy bird of the (14) day.'

This unintelligible passage contains a play on words between *rmj*, 'weeping' (Coptic ⲣⲓⲙⲉ), and *rm*, 'fish' (Coptic, Boh. ⲣⲁⲙⲓ); the last words have indeed passed into a proverb.

The reverse of the tablet was much written over, and in places it is obvious that there have been erasures. In two places were portions of repetitions of the text on the obverse (lines 11, 12), also a list of names in the same handwriting, showing that it was all the work of the same person, like the text on the reverse of 21.

'Three people were concerned—
Amenemheb,
Amen-em-ene,
Amon-neb,
.... (a woman),
.... (a woman),
[Amen]-nekht (a man),
Beki (a man).'

21. Small writing tablet of wood covered with stucco (Pl. LXXVI. 1 and 2). At the left side of the obverse is a hole for a string. The reverse is mended with a piece of bark.

Obverse:—

[1] Probably southern Arabia.
[2] The names following remain visible from the previous inscription.
[3] Read ...
[4] Possibly ...

THE HIERATIC TEXTS OF TOMB NO. 87

The text is badly damaged, the most intelligible is the second line: 'If the boy comes to the barrack if he be weeping ...' Evidently, from first to last, this text concerns a nurse. The reverse contains a list of four names which, as we have already mentioned, occur also in the text of No. 26, and in the same handwriting.

Amenemheb,

Amen-nekht,

Amen-em-ene,

Amen-neb.

CHAPTER XIV

VEGETABLE REMAINS FOUND IN THE EXCAVATIONS
(Pl. LXXIX)

By Percy E. Newberry

Fig. 1. Fig baskets composed of leaves of the Date Palm (*Phoenix dactylifera*, L.).

Fig. 2. A. Some species of Compositae not identified.
      B. Leaves of the Persea tree (*Mimusops Schimperi*, Hochst.).
      C. Leaves of the Grape Vine (*Vitis vinifera*, L.).
      D. Stones of the *Balanites aegyptiaca*, Del.
      E. Fruit of the Persea tree (*Mimusops Schimperi*, Hochst.).
      F. Fruit of the Sycomore Fig (*Ficus Sycomorus*, L.).
      G. Young fruit of the Date Palm (*Phoenix dactylifera*, L.).
      H. Mature fruits of *Balanites aegyptiaca*, Del.

With the exception of the fragments of flower-stalks (Fig. 2 A) of some species of Compositae, the specimens figured here are all of well-known ancient Egyptian plants. Two of them, the *Mimusops Schimperi* and the *Balanites aegyptiaca*, are not now known in Egypt proper.

INDEX

A

Aah-hetep, funerary statuette of, 20.
    called Ta-nezem, 74.
Aahmes, funerary statuette of, 20.
    coffin bearing name of, 84.
    Mayor, 32.
Aahmes-nefert-ari, mother of, 3.
    earliest portrait of, 2.
    wall of, 11, 28.
    bricks of, 11, 30.
Aahmes-sa-pa-ar, funerary statuette of, 20.
Abdu, contemporary of Hyksos kings, referred to, 66.
Adze, model of, 31, 40.
Ahat, 49.
Ah-hotep, letter to, 90.
    treasure of Queen, referred to, 37.
Ahmosi, 37.
Amen-em-ene, 92.
Amenemhat IV, name on casket, 6, 56.
Amenemhat, 29.
Amenemheb, statuette of, 75, 92.
Amenhetep I, wall of, 11, 28.
    bricks of, 11, 30.
    scarab of, 8, 72.
Amenhetep II, brick of, 50.
Amenhetep, scribe of the altar, 29.
Amenhetep-en-auf, 25.
Amen-nekht, 92.
Amen-renpet, overseer of workmen, 50.
Amenti-figures, in wax, 25.
Amphorae, buried under graves, 8, 43.
Amulet, *ka-hetep*, 87.
Amulets, Middle Kingdom, 53.
Amuletic necklaces, 60, 80, 82, 85.
Ana, mother of Kemen, 56.
Ankhu, coffin fragment bearing name of, 52.
Antef, funerary statuette of, 20.
Arrows, fragments of, 87.
Asiatics, mentioned, 36.
Assa, King, mentioned, 36.
Atef, funerary statuette of, 20.
Atef-s-senb, 63.
Auf-aa-hor, Mayor of Thebes, 49.
Auy-res, stela of, 62.
Auy-senb, 63.
Avaris, mentioned, 36.
Axe, model of, 31.

B

Bag, small linen, 76.
Bak-en-Khonsu, royal scribe, 49.
Balanites aegyptiaca, 28, 94.
Bangles, bead, 70, 78, 82, 84, 85, 86.
Baskets, rush-work, 72, 74, 75, 78, 84.
Batten, weaver's, 61.
Beads, Middle Kingdom, 53, 59, 60, 71, 87.
    sprinkled in mummy wrappings, 70.
Bead-work upon leather, 32.
Bedstead (angarib), 51.
Beki, 92.
Birâbi, 4.
Bird-trap, 77.
Black soil, pit filled with, 63.
Bladder-stone found in mummy, 71.
Boat, model of, 51.
Bowl, alabaster, 80, 83.
    faience, 52, 80.
Bracelet, ivory, 81.
Brick, name of, on stone, 41.
Brick-mould, model of, 31.
Brooch, *shen*, 55.
Burials, undisturbed, 10, 23, 24, 86.
    concealed by officials, 65.
    stored in tomb, 64.
    in decorated rectangular coffins, 70, 78, 81, 82.
    in plain rectangular gable-topped coffins, 71, 80, 83, 84, 85, 86.
    in plain rectangular flat-topped coffins, 73, 78, 79, 81, 82, 85, 86.

INDEX

Burials, in plain rectangular grid-bottomed coffins, 79, 80.
    in dug-out coffins, 61, 78.
    in *Rishi* coffins, 70, 71, 82, 83, 84.
    in plain anthropoid coffins, 70, 78, 79.
    in semi-decorated anthropoid coffins, 70, 83.
    in decorated anthropoid coffins, 73, 74, 84, 85.
    children's, 26, 78, 79, 80, 81, 82, 83, 86.
    reed, 50.
    rush, 34, 50.

C

Campbell, Rev. Dr. Collin, 26.
Canopic box, 35; jar lid, 61.
Carnarvon Papyri, I and II, 43, 46.
    Tablets, I, II, III, IV, 4, 34, 36, 70, 77, 78, 90, 92.
Casket, ivory, ebony, and cedar-wood, 6, 7, 54, 55.
Castanets, ivory, 86, 87.
Chairs, 50, 72.
Chignon, 84.
Chisel, of chert, 10.
    model of, 31.
Circular pit, 63.
Coffins of Heq-Tau, referred to, 67.
    decorated rectangular, 66.
    rectangular with gable top, 66.
        with flat top, 67.
        with grid bottoms, 67.
    'dug-out', 30, 61, 68.
    Rishi, 60, 62, 68.
    anthropoid, plain, 68.
    decorated anthropoid, 25, 68.
    children's, 26, 69.
Coinage, preservation of, in Upper Egypt, 44.
Coins, Ptolemaic, 8, 43, 44.
Combs, 82, 84, 85.
Cones, pottery, 10, 22, 24.
Copts, dwelling in tombs, 9, 22.
Cowroid seals, 32, 71, 78, 80, 82, 85.
Crucible, for smelting metal, model of, 36.
Cynocephalous ape, clay figure of, 76.

D

Dancers, *MW-*, 17.
Date-cakes, in amphora, 43.
Dedut-res, 63.
Demotic ostraca, 47.
    papyri, 8, 43, 46.

Dice, 58.
Dog, playing piece of a game, 56.
Dôm-palm nuts, 81.
Doorways closed and sealed, 23, 24, 65.
Draught-board, 36.
Dwellings for workmen, 11, 29.
    for embalmers, 27.

E

Earrings, gold, 80, 86.
Edgar, Mr., referred to, 42.
Epiphanes, Ptolemaios, 8, 46.
Erde-en-ptah, 63.
Erman, Prof., referred to, 26, 90.
Ethiopia, mentioned, 36.
Euergetes I, 47.
Excavations, at Birâbi, 4, 34.
    at Dêr el Bahari, 9, 22.
    near village mosque, 2.

F

Fan, handle and clasp of, 72.
Feretories for animals, 49.
Fig-baskets, 33.
Fillet of copper, 87.
    gold, 55.
    leaves, 25.
Forceps, 61, 72, 74.
Foundation deposits: Dêr el Bahari dromos, 4, 30, 33.
    implements placed separate, 31.
    of Rameses IV, 9, 48.
    of tomb, 28.
    of 'valley'-temple, 4, 39.
Frog, steatite, glazed, 52.
Funerary statuettes, discovered in position, 3, 13, 19.
    as guardians to tomb, 13, 19.
    found in tomb of Teta-ky, 19.

G

Gaming-board, 7, 56.
Gardiner, Mr. A. H., referred to, 36.
Gemmez (sycomore-fig), 11.
Girdle, bead, 85.
Glue, 56, 57.
'Good' festival mentioned on stone blocks, 41.
Grain in foundation deposit, 30, 38, 48.
Graver, model of, 31.

INDEX

H

Hair, locks of, 72, 84.
    plaited, 55, 84, 85.
Hair-pin of ivory, 84.
Hammers of chert, 10.
Harmachis, King, 46.
Harmose, letter of, 90.
Hathor cow, 3, 16.
Hatshepsût, Queen, bricks stamped with her name, 40.
    'valley'-temple of, 4.
    tally-stone of, 40.
    scarab of, 8, 73.
    Nebti-name of, on deposit, 31.
    measured temple for Amon, 31.
    foundation deposits, 30, 33, 40.
Head-rests, 61, 67, 71, 81, 84.
Hent, 7.
Henut, the Lady, 55.
Henŷt, coffin fragment of, 87.
Hieroglyphs, mutilated, 55, 61.
Hoe, 40; model of, 31.
Hone for sharpening, 72, 83.
Hor, Priest of Amen, 49.
Hor-kheb, priest, 49.
Hor-se-Ast, Governor of Thebes, 49.
Horus, variant sign for, 85.
Hounds *contra* jackals, the game of, 58.
Hu-uben-ef, statuette of, 75.
Hyksos scarabs, 8, 72, 79.
    tablet relating to expulsion of, from Egypt, 4, 37.

I

Ihŷ, stela of, 89.
Implements, models of, in deposit, 5, 30, 31, 40.
Inscriptions on stone blocks, 39, 40.
    on vase, 90.
Instrument of wood, 76.
Ivory, bracelet of, 81.
    on toilet-box, 55.
    gaming-board, 56.
    castanets, 86, 87.

J

Jackals, playing pieces, 56.
Jar-rest, model of, 31.
Jar-seals, 32.

Jewel-boxes, 53, 80, 87.
Jones, Mr. Cyril, 30.

K

Ka-hetep amulet, 87.
Kamosi, King, 4, 86.
Kati-nekht, canopic box of, 35.
Kemen, 'keeper of the food department,' 56.
Keriba, statuette of, 29.
Kha-em-hat, bas-relief from tomb of, 10.
Khety, coffin of, 52.
Knuckle-bones, 58, 76.
Kohl-box, 72.
Kohl-pot, 72, 83, 84, 85, 87.
Kohl-stick, 72, 74, 84.
Ky-nefer, shawabti figure of, 32.

L

Leaf offerings, 11.
Linen, mended mummy-wrappings, 26.
Linen purse, 76.
Lion, fragment of, in faience, 52.
Lock of hair in basket, 84.

M

Maartu, coffin and mummy of, 24, 25.
Mallet, mason's, 40.
    model of, 31.
Maspero, Sir Gaston, referred to, 10.
Mechanical toy, 78.
Memphis, 36.
Men-hetep, name on pot, 52.
Mentu-hetep, 30.
    stones from temple of King, 4.
    coffin bearing name of, 85.
Mes-per, the Lady, 49.
Mezaiu (Nubians), mentioned, 37.
Mirrors, 7, 55, 72, 84.
Mortar-bed in tomb, 71.
Mummy-wrappings, 25, 69, 70.
    embroidered, 25.
    worn and mended, 25, 26.
Musical instruments, 70.
    stringed, 77, 82, 87.
    reed-pipes, 84.
MW-dancers, depicted in tomb-painting, 17.

N

Nanu-nes-her, the Lady, 25.
Naville, Prof., referred to, 68.
Nebbek-tree, fruits of, 31, 86.
Neb-ded-ra, scarab of, 81.
Necklaces, 7, 55, 59, 60, 71, 78, 80, 81, 86.
Necropolis, Middle Kingdom and Intermediate Period, 5, 51.
Nefer-ur, shawabti figure of, 50.
Neferu-ra, scarab of Princess, 8, 80.
Nekht-ef-mut, priest, 49.
Nekhtu, funerary statuette of, 20.
Nenen, scribe of the army, 61.
Nes-Khonsu-pa-khred, 49.
Nes-ta-nebt-Asheru, the Lady, 49.
Nicol, Mr. Erskine E., 68.

O

Obsidian, 7, 55, 60, 78.
Offerings to trees, 11, 29.
    dates, 49.
    flesh and blood, 5, 30, 31.
    flower, 24.
    leaf, 11, 49.
    votive, 11.
Office of clerk of the works of Dêr el Bahari Temple, 29.
Ornaments for mummy-wrappings, 53.
Osiride figure, 50.
Ox, bones of, 31.

P

Pachnumis, 46.
Pa-de-Amen, coffin of, 24.
    genealogy of, 26.
Pa-de-khonsu, 24.
    coffin of, 25.
Pa-khnems, funerary statuette of, 20.
Palette, scribe's, 52, 61, 76.
Palm-tree, in front of tomb, 27.
    design on gaming-board, 57.
Pan-pottery, 77.
Panel stelae, 70, 87, 89.
Paos, 46.
Papyrus, demotic, 43, 46.
    hieratic, 30.
    reeds, 78.
Pedemut, priest, 49.
Peg, model of, 31.

Pepa, 37.
Petamenophis, public notary, 46.
Petemestus, 46.
Petrie, Prof. Flinders, referred to, 68.
Philadelphos, 47.
P-ohi-n-p-mehen, 46.
Pomade (pomatum), 69, 84.
Portcullis to sarcophagus chamber, 22.
Pottery, XIth Dyn., 28.
    Middle Kingdom, 53, 60.
    Intermediate Period, 87.
    XVIIth Dyn., 35.
    XVIIIth Dyn., 31, 32.
Proverbs of Ptah-hetep, 4, 36.
Psenesis, herdsman, 46.
Ptolemaic coins, 44.
Pu-am-ra, hieratic inscriptions of, 4, 39.

Q

Quibell, Mr. J. E., referred to, 58.

R

Ra-hotep, funerary statuette of, 19, 20.
Rameses IV, colonnade, 8, 9, 48.
    foundation deposit, 9, 48.
    variants of cartouches of, 48.
Razor, copper, 78, 83.
Reed-burial, 50.
Reed-pen case, 75.
Relatives of Teta-ky, 19.
Ren-senb, coffin of, 7, 54.
    mirror of, 55.
    scarab of the herald, 69, 74.
Res, funerary statuette of, 19, 20.
Reth-ar-es, 25.
Rhind, Mr., referred to, 10.
Rishi coffins, 7, 17, 32, 60, 62, 68.
    model coffin like, 50.
Roast meat, the word for, in hieratic, 31.
Rope of Dôm-palm fibre, 71.
Rush-burial, 50.

S

Sacrifice, animal, 28.
Sa-Hathor, 63.
Saite burials, undisturbed, 10, 23.
Sale agreements, 46, 47.
Sandals, 28, 72.
Satin, 37.

INDEX

Scarab-seals, tied on arm, 26.
    position when worn as ring, 70.
    of Middle Kingdom, 7, 53.
    XIIIth Dyn., 8.
    Amenhetep I, 72.
    Thothmes I, 81.
    Thothmes II, 81.
    Thothmes III, 80.
    Neferu-ra, 8, 80.
    Neb-ded-ra, 81.
    Ren-senb, 74.
    of red jasper, 73, 80.
    of green jasper, 72.
    of blue paste, 74.
    of green paste, 80.
    of steatite, glazed, 26, 53, 78, 80, 81, 82, 83, 85, 87.
    of steatite, unburnt, 74.
    of amethyst, 53.
Sceptre, bronze snake, 85.
Scribe's outfit, 70, 75.
Sealed doorway in tomb, 65.
Sebek, Lord of Illahun, 7, 56.
Sebek-hetep, *Uab*-priest, 63.
Sedemt, 50.
Sena, funerary statuette of, 20.
Senba, the Lady, 15.
Senbu, funerary statuette of, 19, 20.
Senmut, name of, on stone block, 4, 41.
Sen-senb, funerary statuette of, 19, 20.
Sep-en-urdet, the Lady, 63.
Sent, the Lady, 55.
Sent-sign on stone blocks, 41.
Sent-nw-pw, the Lady, 63.
Serpentine wall, 30.
Sheikh Abd El Kurneh, tomb of, 11.
Shrines for animals, 49.
Sieves, models of, 31.
Sinaitic ibex, sketch of, 32.
Sites excavated, 2.
Slab for washing, 30.
Sledge, mummy depicted upon a, 17.
Smelting crucibles for metals, 31.
Snake sceptre, 85.
Sphinx, bronze, 76.
Staff, walking, 74, 81, 83.
Statuettes, 21, 23, 29, 52, 75, 87.
Stones from Dêr el Bahari temple, 9.
    Mentu-hetep's temple, 4.
Stool, wicker-work, 29.
    wooden, 71, 72, 79.
Structure of mud brick unknown, 64.

T

Ta-aa, the Lady, 49.
Ta-bak-en-ta-Ashat-qa, 49.
Table of offerings, 21.
Tahuti, funerary statuette of, 20.
    coffin bearing name of, 74.
Tahutimes, funerary statuette of, 21.
Tahutʃ-aah, funerary statuette of, 21.
Ta-nezem (see Aah-hetep).
Tekenu, transport of, depicted, 17.
Teta, son of Pepa, 37.
Teta, funerary statuette of, 21.
Teta-an, funerary statuette of, 19, 21.
Teta-ankh, funerary statuette of, 21.
Teta-em-ra, funerary statuette of, 19, 21.
Teta-hemt, funerary statuette of, 21.
    mother of Aahmes-nefert-ari, 3, 16.
Teta-ky, tomb of, 2, 12, 14.
    Mayor of Thebes, 21.
    funerary statuettes of, 21.
    table of offerings of, 21.
Teta-mesu, funerary statuette of, 21.
Teta-nefer, funerary statuette of, 19, 21.
Teta-sa, funerary statuette of, 21.
Teta-senb, funerary statuette of, 21.
Thothmes I, brick of, 40.
    scarabs of, 8, 81.
    seals of, on doorway, 8, 65.
Thothmes II, scarabs, 8, 81.
Thothmes III, brick of, 50.
    receiving nourishment from tree, 11.
    scarabs of, 8, 80.
Throw-stick, 80.
Toilet-box, 55.
Tombs re-used in Intermediate Period, 6.
Torso, in limestone, 33.
Tortoise-shell, 76.
Toy, child's, 32.
    mechanical, 78.
Turtle, amulet, 82.

U

Unguent vase, 48.
Unguents in foundation deposit, 5, 30.
Userhat, royal scribe, 29.

V

'Valley'-temple, 4, 38.
Vases, alabaster, 56, 85.

Vases, black pottery, 81, 82, 85.
    inscribed, 81, 90.
Vaulted graves, Ptolemaic, 8, 42.
Vegetable remains, 94.
Vine leaves, 70.
Viscera boxes, 69, 73, 84.
Votive offerings, 11.

W

Walking staff, 74, 81, 83.
Weaver's batten, 61.
Weights, 76.
Wheat, 27.
Wigs, 55, 70, 84.
Wine, 31.

Workmen's washing slab, 30.
Wrappings, mummy, 25, 69, 70.
Wristlet, bead, 86.
Writing tablets, 70, 77, 78, 90, 92.

Y

Ŷma, funerary statuette of, 19, 20.
Ŷ-meru, 68.

Z

Zed-Aah, 49.
Zed-Amen-auf-ankh, stela of, 49.
Zed-Amen-uah-es, 49.
Zed-Khensu-auf-ankh, shawabti figure of, 32.
Zeser-zeseru, 4, 31, 40.

THEBES   PLATE I

Tomb of Teta-Ky

1. Open Court-yard

2. Vaulted Chambers

PAINTED VAULTED CHAMBER · ASCENDING PASSAGE

VAULTED CHAMBER

VAULTED CHAMBER

OPEN COURT-YARD

PIT

NICHES FOR SHAWABTIS IN SARCOPHAGI

TWO FIGURES IN SARCOPHAGI EACH SIDE

PAINTED NICHE

PLAN OF THE TOMB OF TETAKY

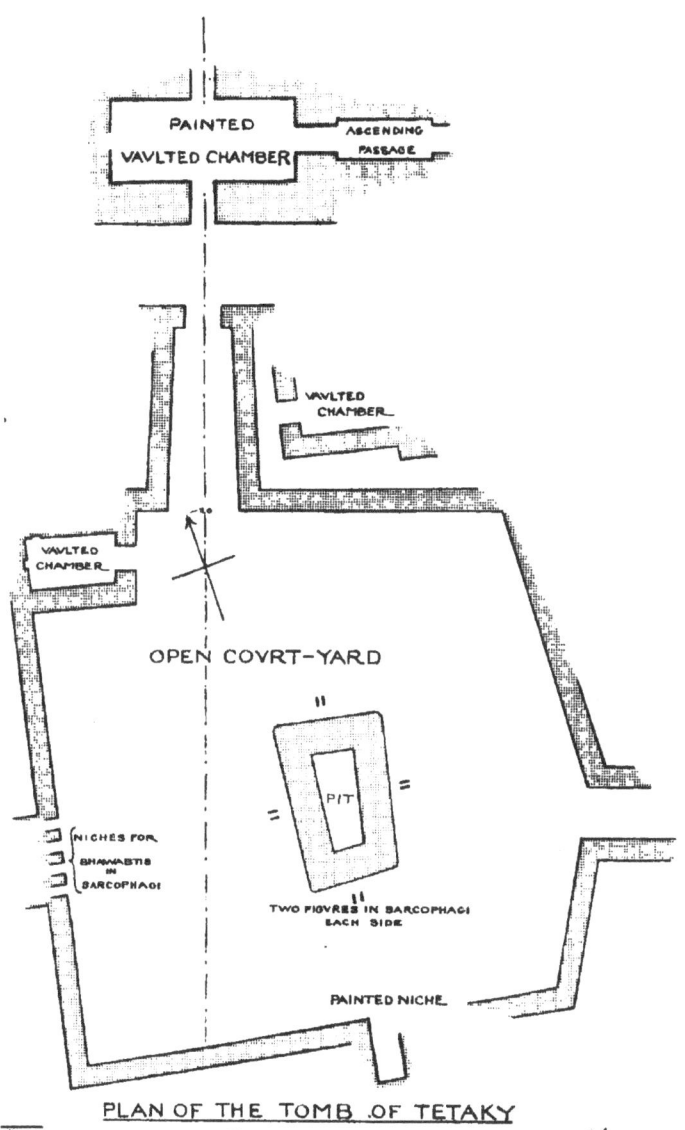

= MUD-BRICKWORK [BRICKS 44×16×12 c/m]   SCALE 1/150

THEBES   PLATE III

TOMB OF TETA-KY

1. RIGHT WALL OF PAINTED NICHE

2. LEFT WALL OF PAINTED NICHE

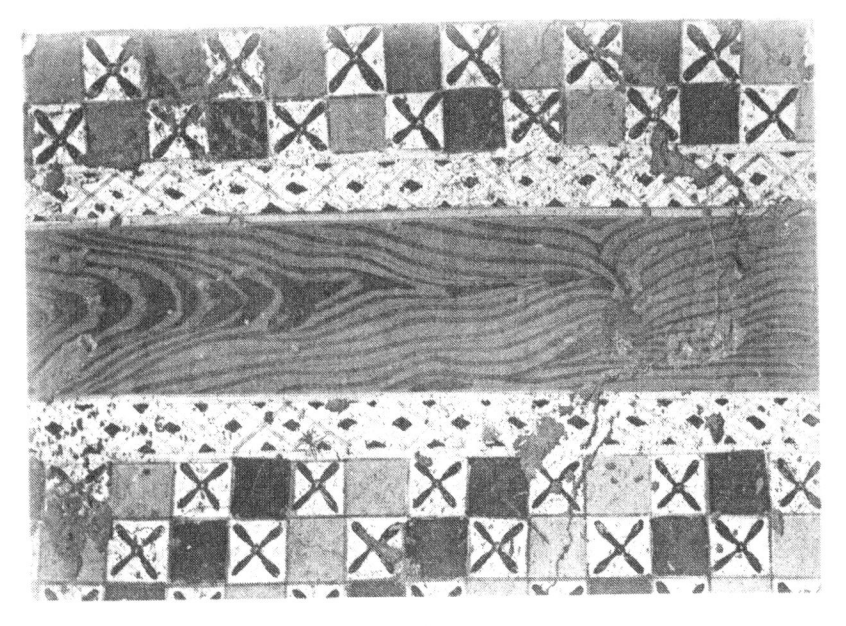

1. Ceiling Decoration

2. Ceiling Decoration and Frieze

THEBES PLATE V

TOMB OF TETA-KY

1. NORTH WALL. SCENES A AND B

2. NORTH WALL. SCENE D

1. EASTERN WALL

2. WESTERN WALL

1. SOUTHERN WALL. SCENE A

2. SOUTHERN WALL. SCENE A (continued)

1. SOUTHERN WALL. SCENE A (*continued*)

2. SOUTHERN WALL SCENE B

TOMB OF TETA-KY

1. SOUTHERN WALL. SCENE C

2. SOUTHERN WALL. SCENES C AND D

THEBES PLATE X

TOMB OF TETA-KY

1. SHAWABTI FIGURE IN MODEL COFFIN

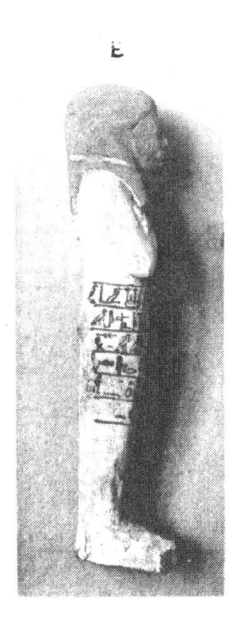

2. SHAWABTI FIGURE OF SEN-SENB

Plain Wood Model Coffins

Plain Mud Model Coffins

Decorated Mud Model Coffins

Inscribed Mud Model Coffins

THEBES — TOMB OF TETA-KY — PLATE XII

1. TABLE FOR OFFERINGS

2. FUNERARY STATUETTES

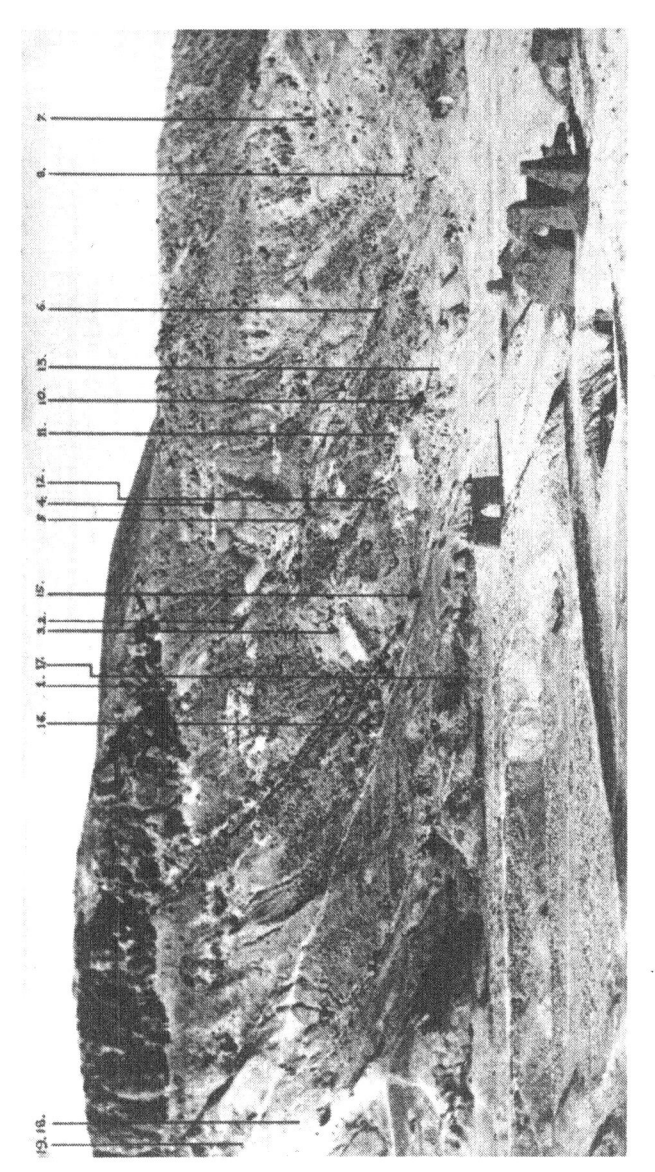

PANORAMIC VIEW SHOWING THE SITES EXCAVATED IN THE DÊR EL BAHARI VALLEY

THEBES
PLATE XIV

DÊR EL BAHARI VALLEY

Tomb No. 5 before Opening

Tomb No. 5 after Opening

THEBES   PLATE XV

DÊR EL BAHARI VALLEY

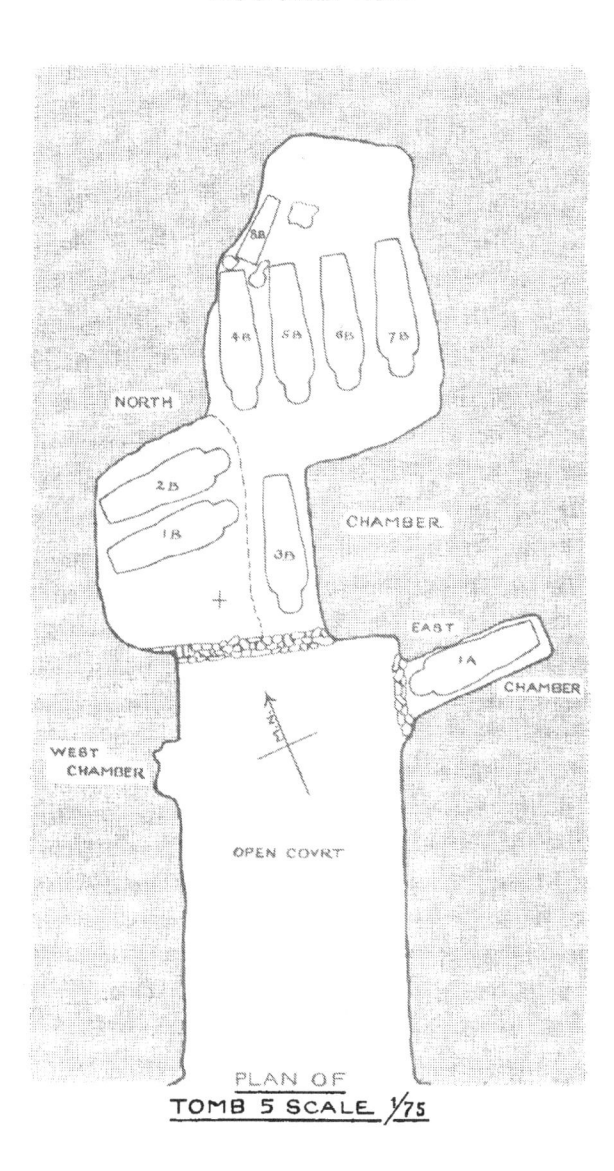

PLAN OF
TOMB 5 SCALE 1/75

FIG. 1. COFFIN NO. 1B

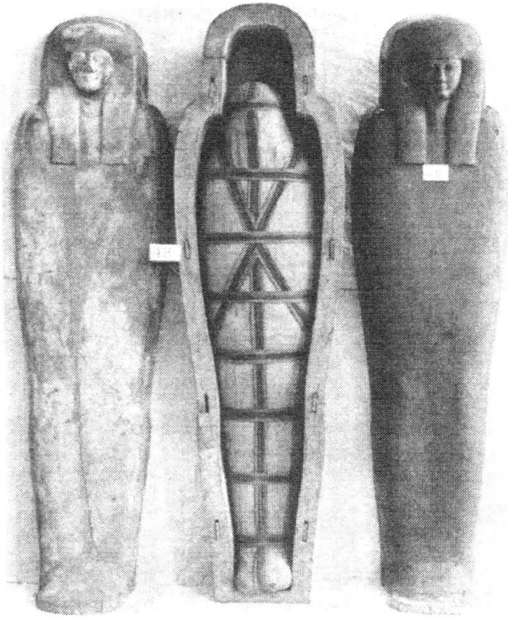

FIG. 2. COFFINS NOS. 3B AND 4B

FIG. 3. COFFIN NO. 1A

SERIES OF COFFINS FROM TOMB NO. 5

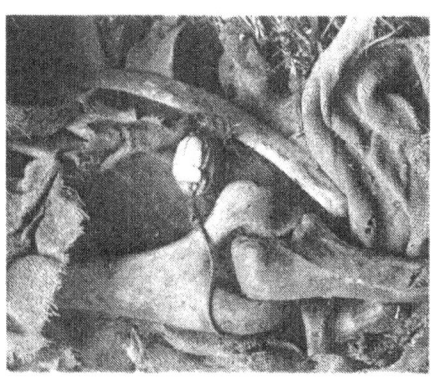

1. SCARAB ON MUMMY ARM. (TOMB NO. 5)

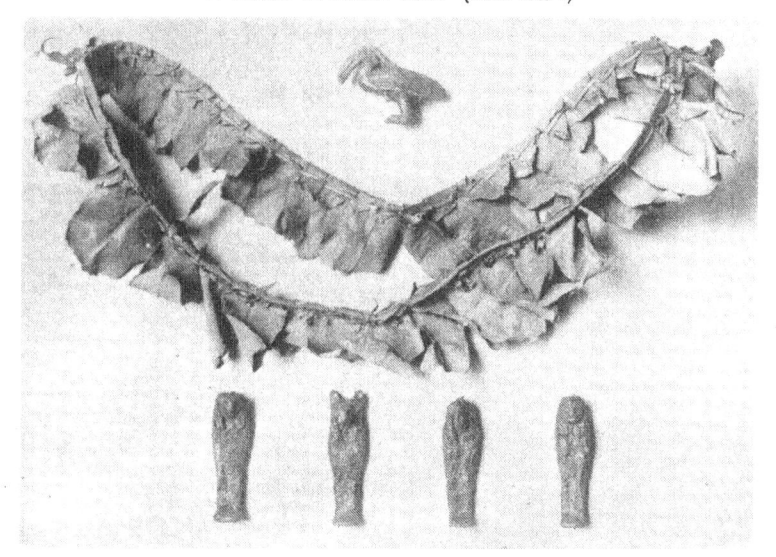

2. WREATH AND WAX AMULETS. (TOMB NO. 5)

3. COFFIN *in situ.* (TOMB NO. 5)

1 & 2. Limestone Statuette. (Tomb No. 4)

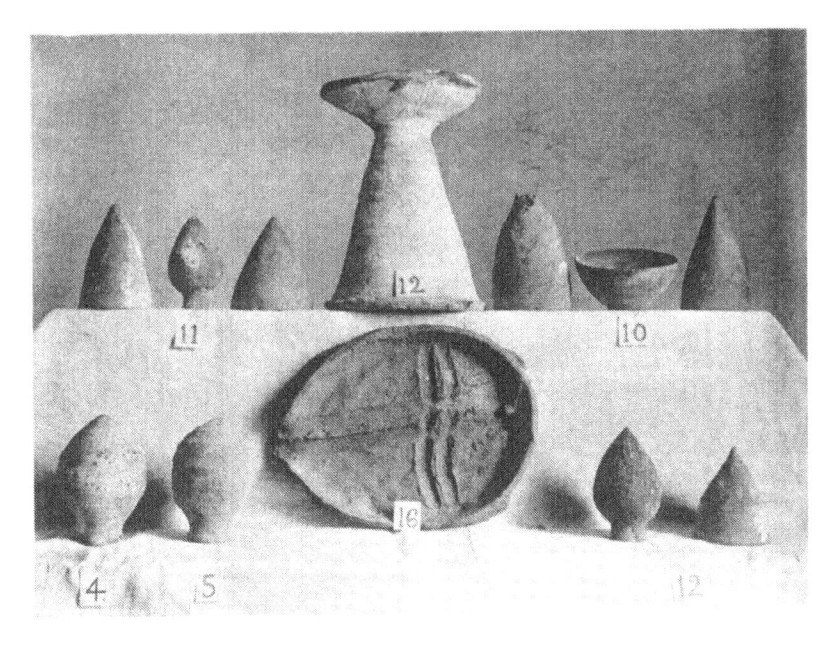

3. Pottery from Tombs Nos. 1–16

Dêr el Bahari Valley

1. Foundations of Wall of Amenhetep I and Aahmes-nefert-ari, and Workmen's Dwellings

2. Offerings to a Tree

THEBES PLATE XX

DÊR EL BAHARI VALLEY

1. 'SERPENTINE' WALL

2. BATHING SLAB

THEBES Dêr el Bahari Valley PLATE XXI

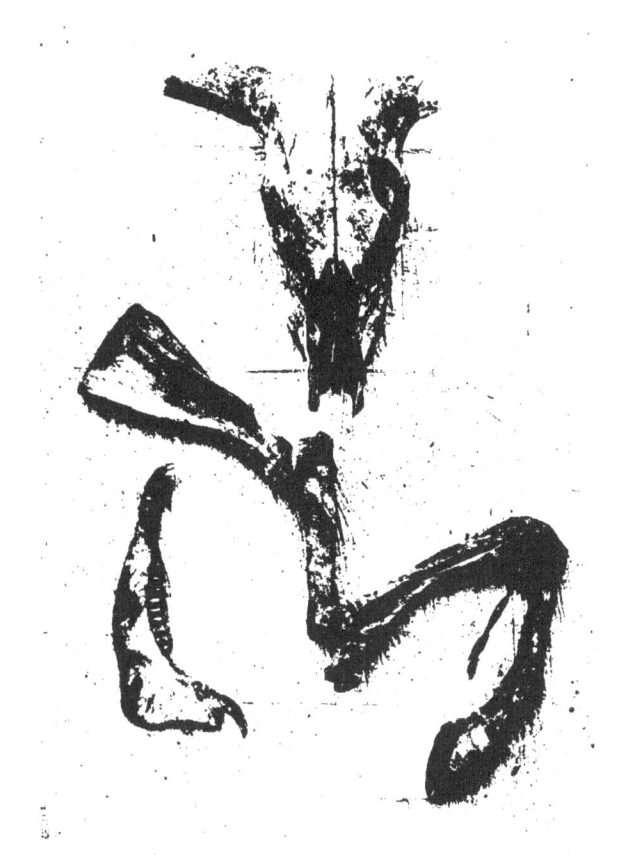

1. OFFERINGS FROM THE DROMOS DEPOSIT

2. BRICK-LINED HOLE MADE FOR THE DROMOS DEPOSIT

THEBES PLATE XXII

Dêr el Bahari Valley

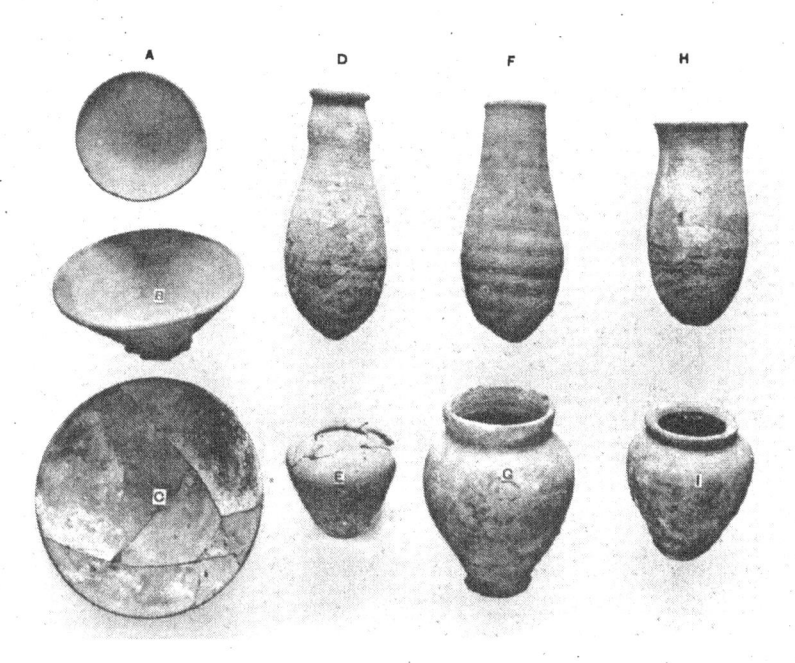

1. Pottery from the Dromos Deposit

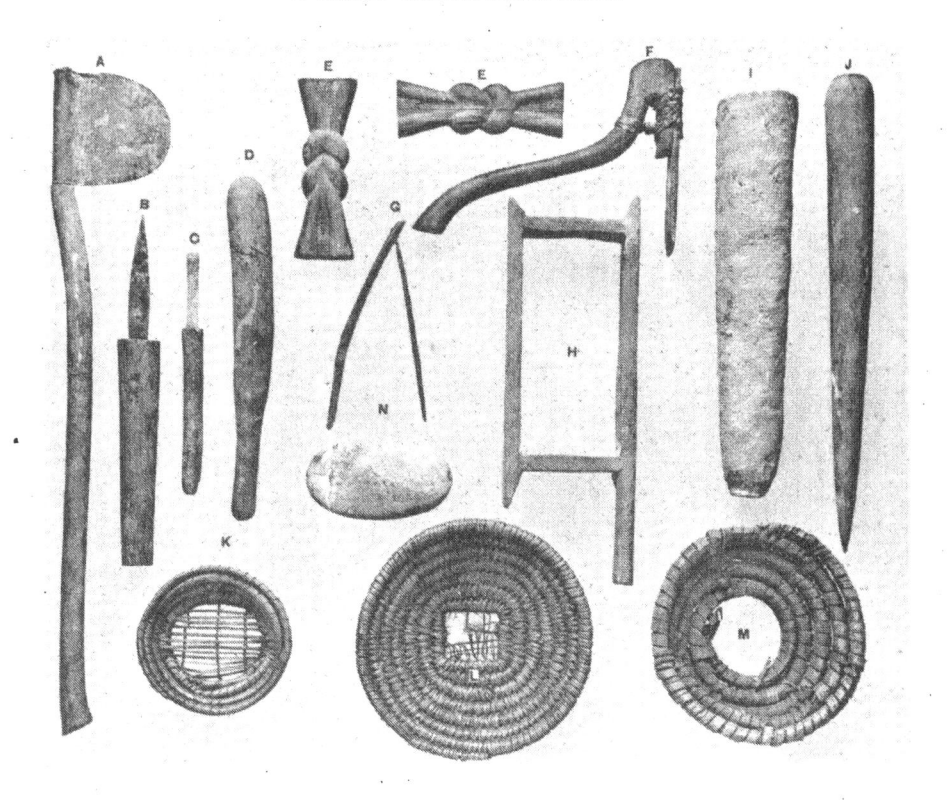

2. Implements from the Dromos Deposit

1. Child's Toy

2. Pottery from Excavations

3. Stamped Bricks of Amenhetep I and Aahmes-Nefert-Ari

PANORAMIC VIEW OF DÊR EL BAHARI VALLEY

A. Site of 'Valley'-Temple.   B & C. Dromos Deposits

Tomb No. 9

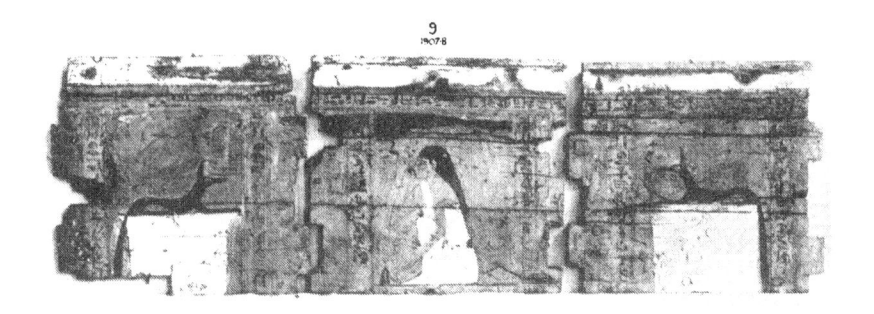

1. Three Sides of a Canopic Box

2. Three Canopic Jars in Pottery

1

2

Pottery from Tomb No. 9

Tomb No. 9

Carnarvon Tablet I. Obv.

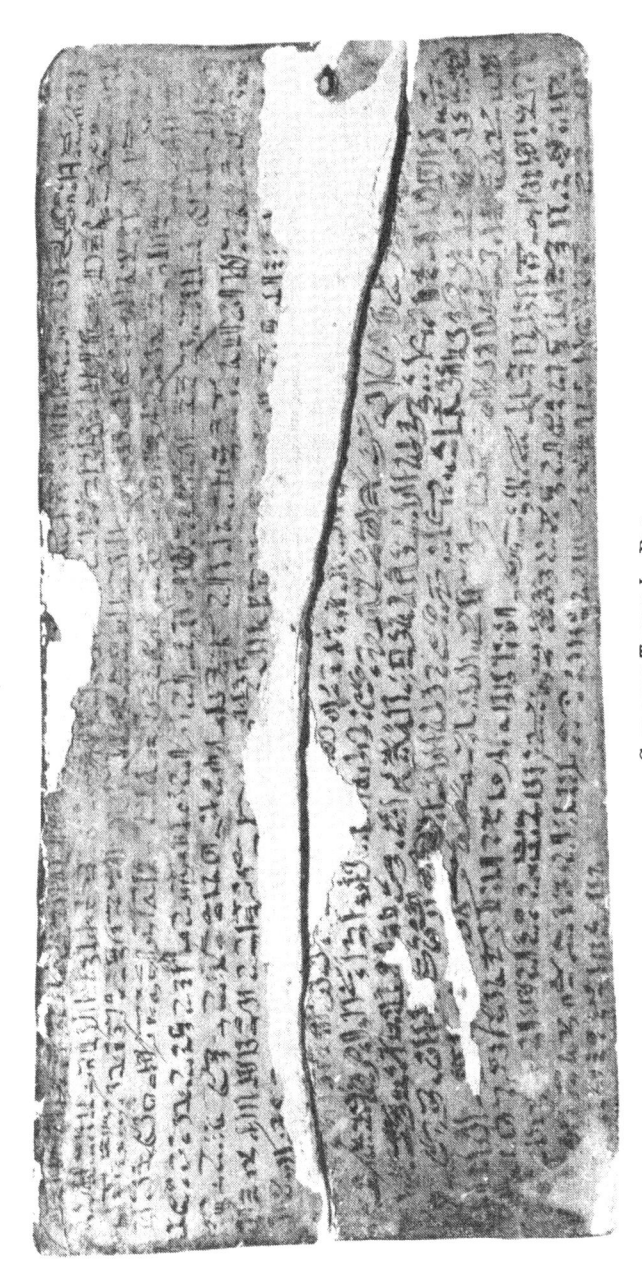

Tomb No. 9

Carnarvon Tablet I. Rev.

Tomb No. 9

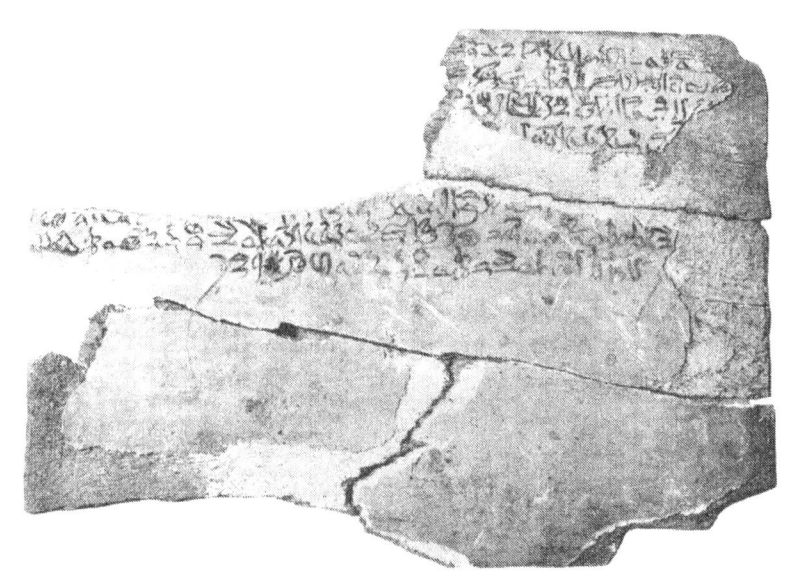

1. Carnarvon Tablet II. Obv.

2. Carnarvon Tablet II. Rev.

PLAN OF HATSHEPSÛT'S 'VALL

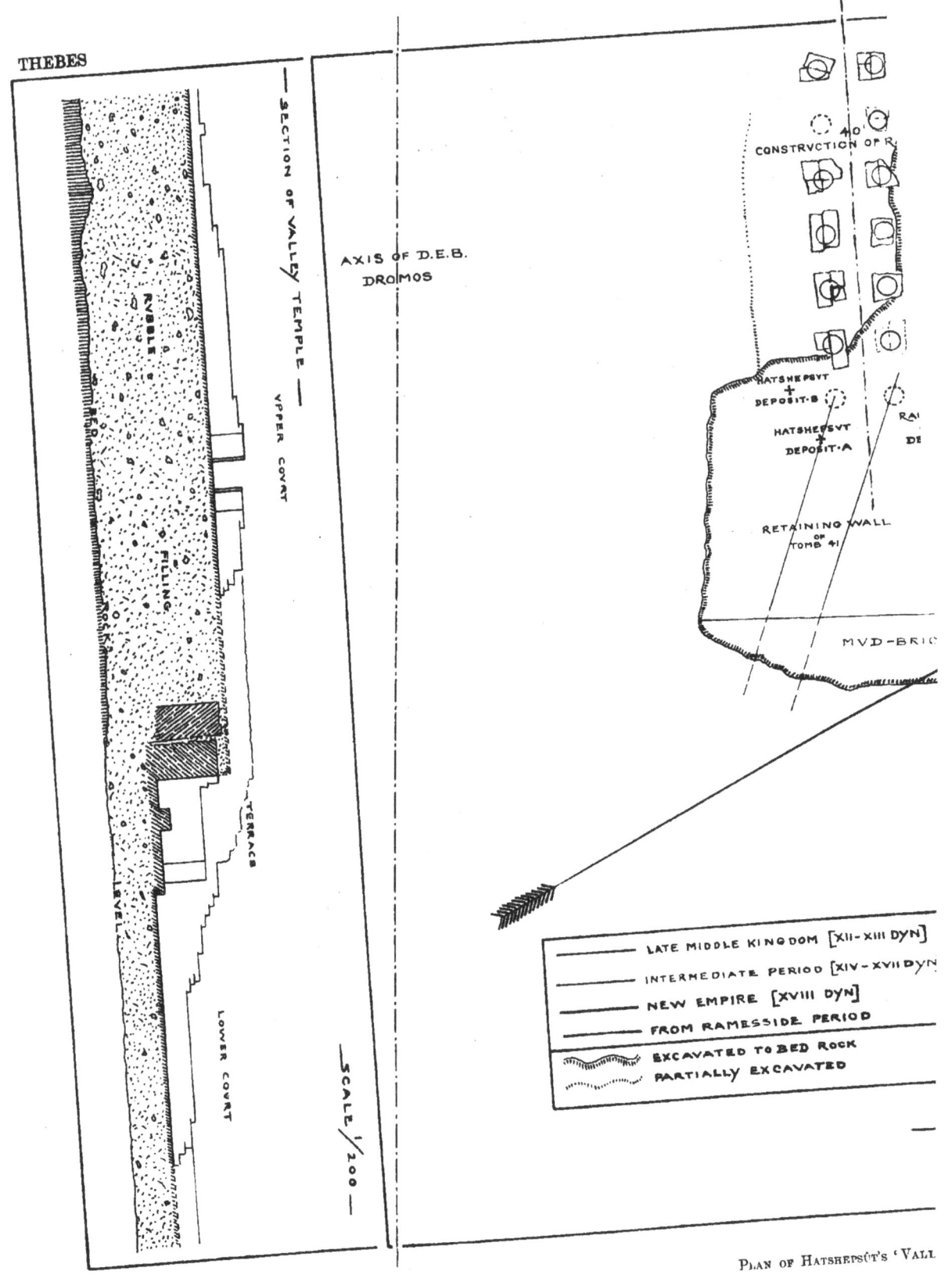

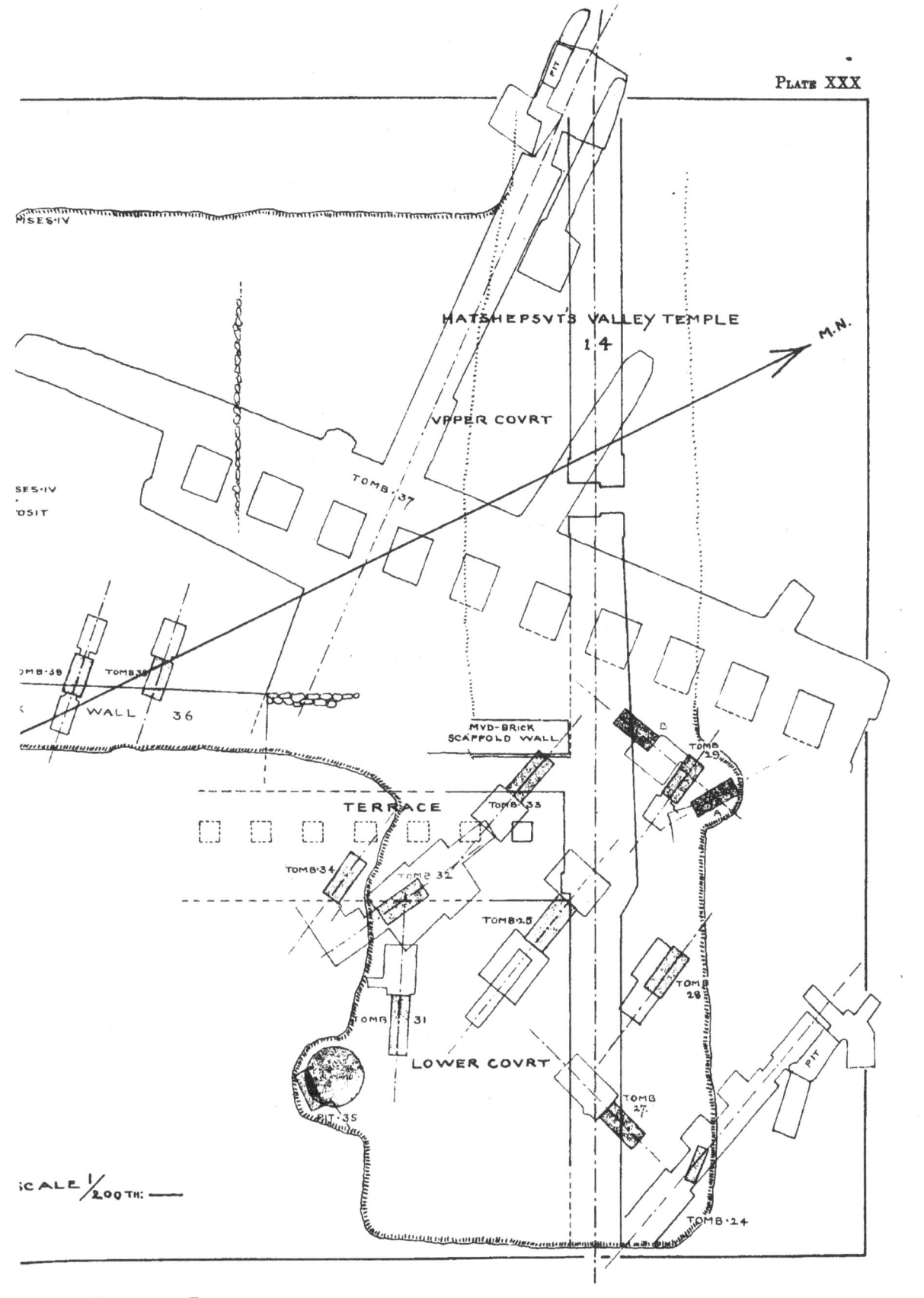

PLATE XXX

HATSHEPSUT'S VALLEY TEMPLE
14

UPPER COURT

M.N.

TOMB·37

TOMB·38
WALL 36

MUD-BRICK
SCAFFOLD WALL

TOMB·29

TERRACE
TOMB·33

TOMB·34 TOMB·32

TOMB·25

TOMB·31   TOMB·28

LOWER COURT

PIT·35 TOMB·27

PIT

TOMB·24

SCALE 1/200TH:

...MPLE AND NEIGHBOURING TOMBS

THEBES
Hatshepsût's 'Valley'-Temple
Plate XXXI

1

2

1 & 2.   Northern Boundary Wall of 'Valley'-Temple

HATSHEPSÛT'S 'VALLEY'-TEMPLE   PLATE XXXII

1. TALLY-STONE OF HATSHEPSÛT

2. STAMPED BRICK OF QUEEN HATSHEPSÛT

3. WOODEN HOE

4. STAMPED BRICKS OF HATSHEPSÛT AND THOTHMES I

PTOLEMAIC VAULTED GRAVES

VIEW OF PTOLEMAIC VAULTED GRAVES OVER SITE NO. 14

1. Amphorae beneath Floor of Vaulted Grave

2. Façade of Vaulted Grave

THEBES

PTOLEMAIC VAULTED GRAVES

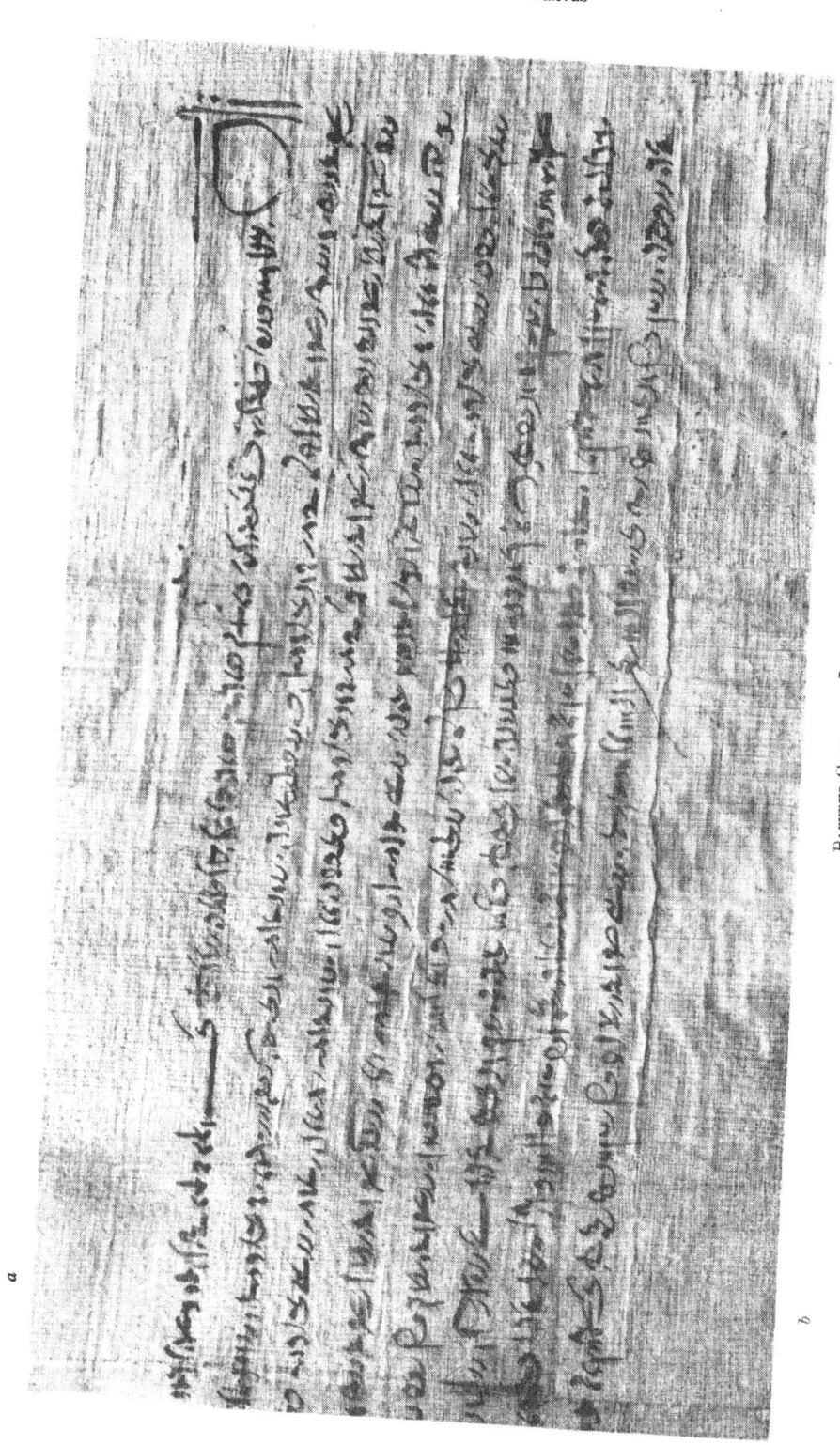

PLATE XXXV

PAPYRUS CARNARVON I

a

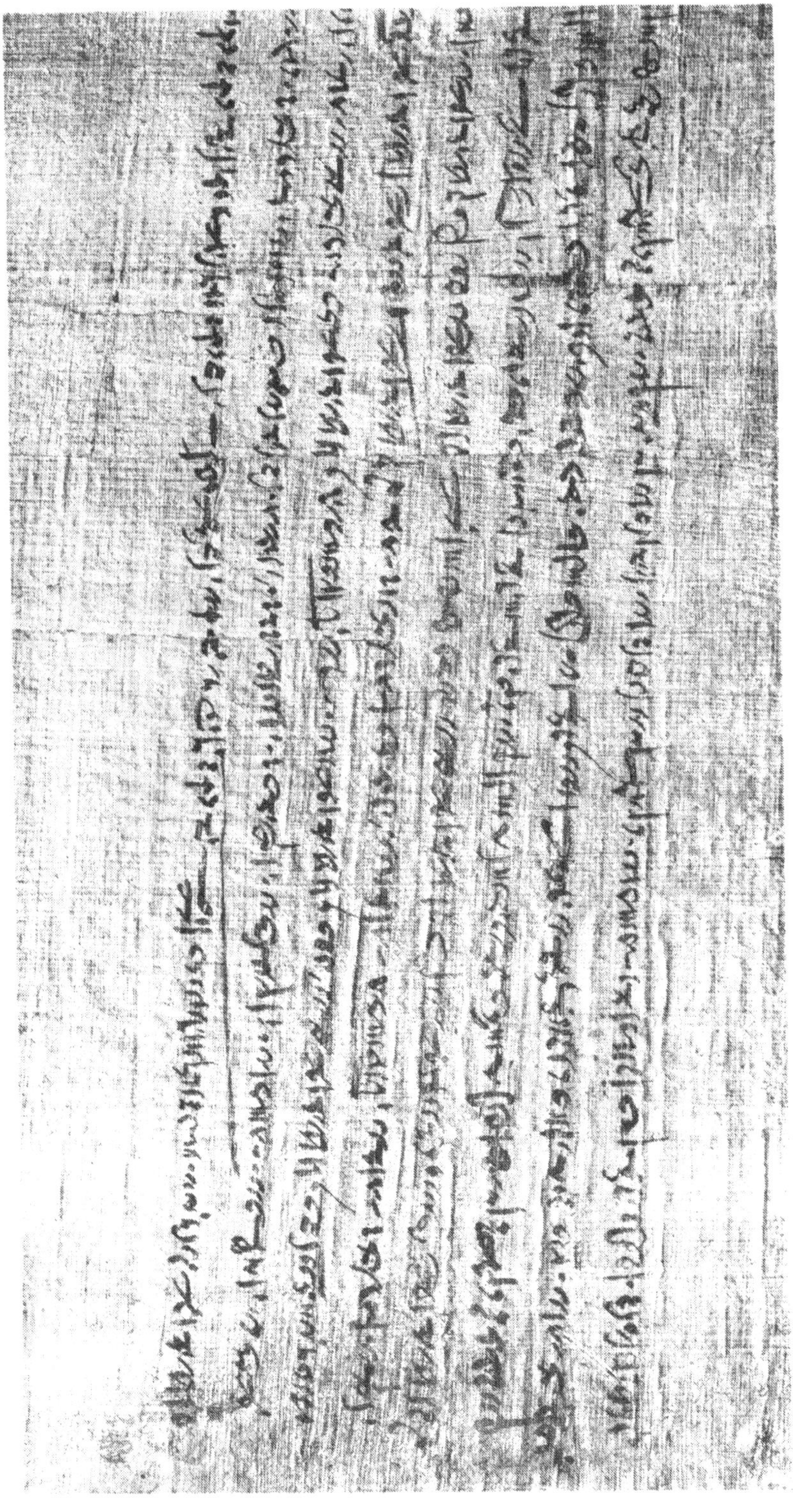

b

PAPYRUS CARNARVON I (*continued from* PLATE XXXV)

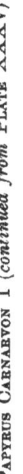

2. DOCKET OF PAPYRUS

3. INSCRIBED POTSHERD

1. DOCKET OF PAPYRUS

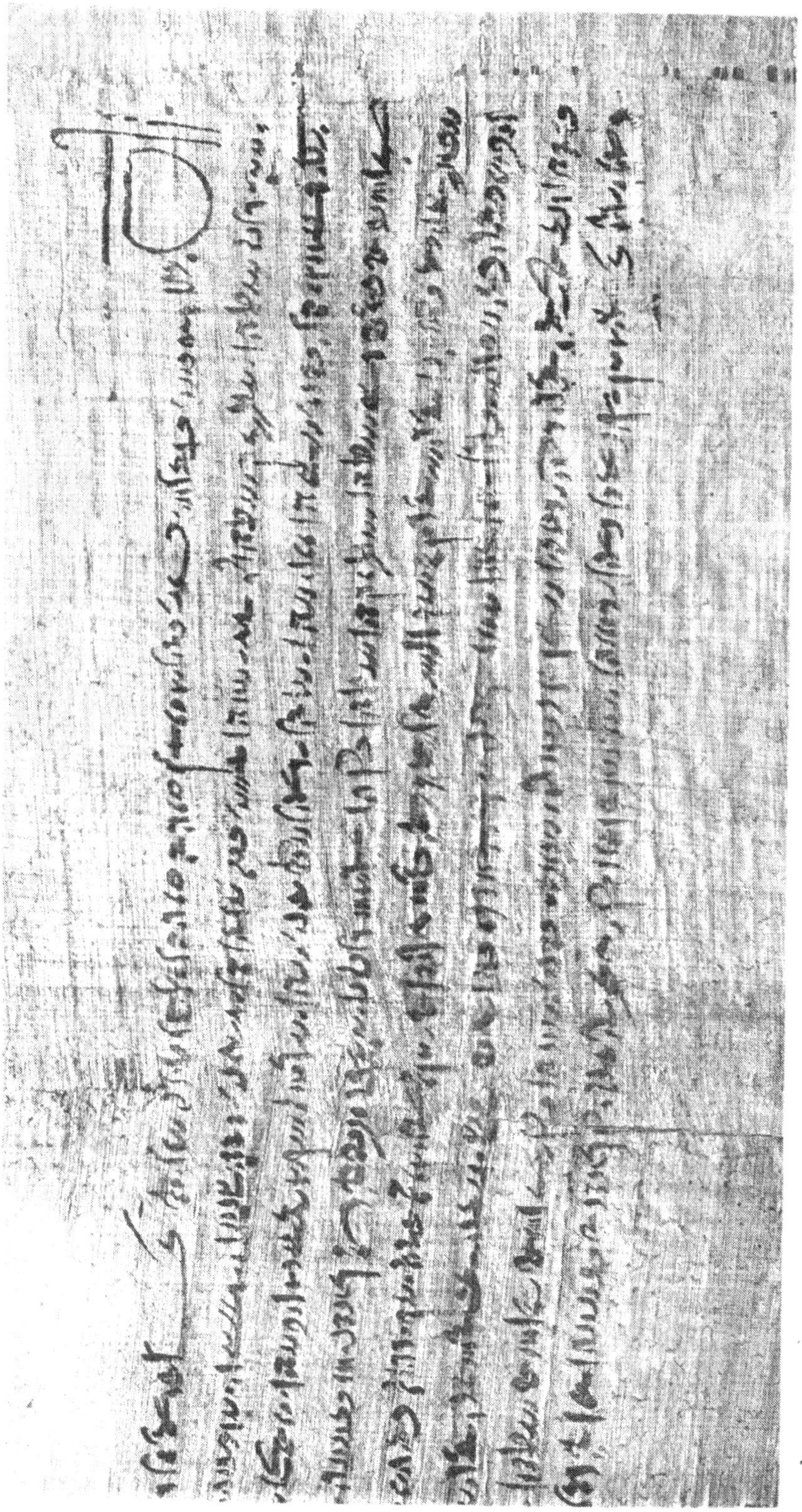

a

b

PAPYRUS CARNARVON II

PTOLEMAIC VAULTED GRAVES

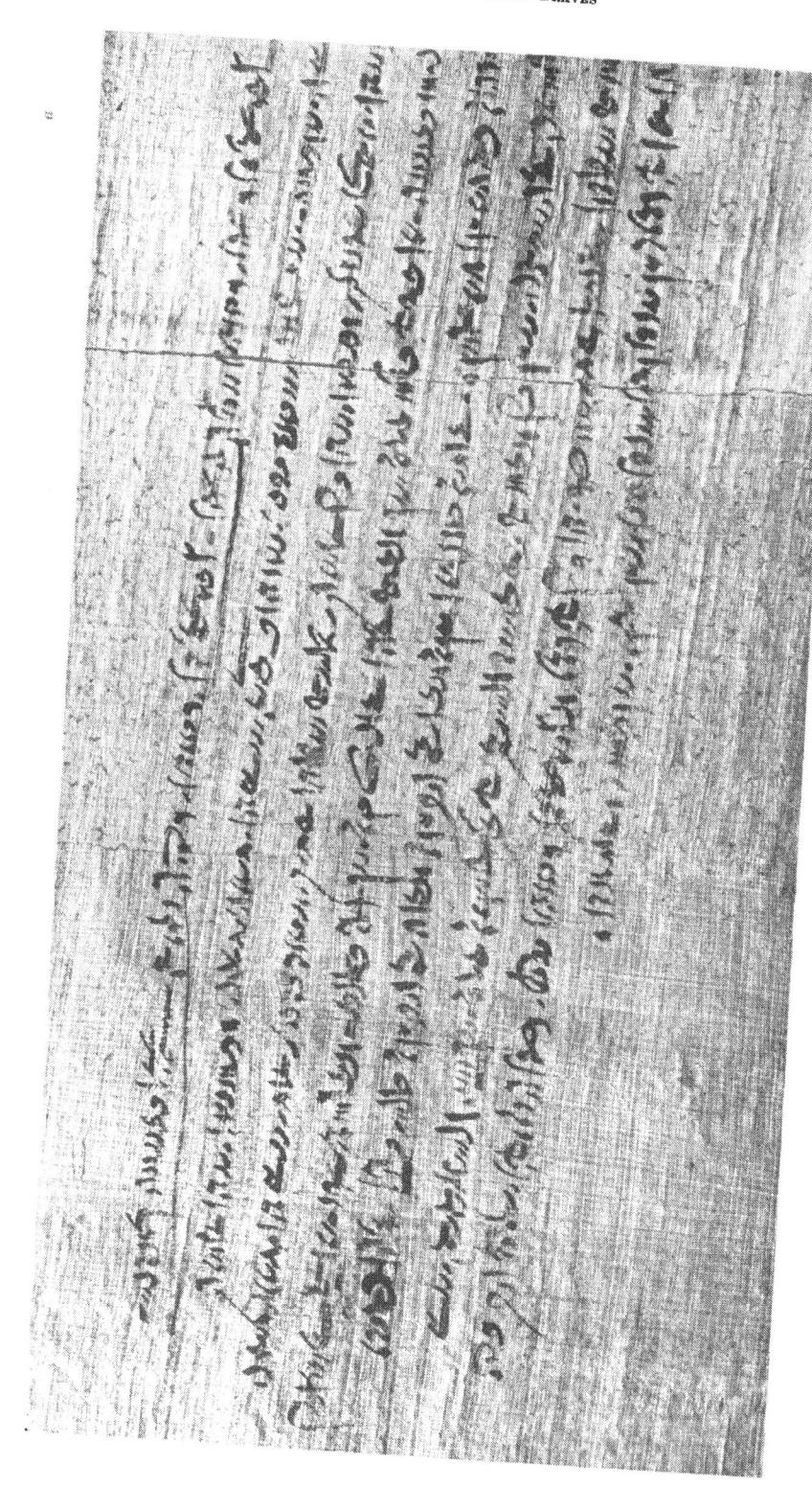

PAPYRUS CARNARVON II (continued from PLATE XXXVIII)

Site No. 40

Foundation Deposit of Rameses IV

SITE No. 14

XXIInd DYNASTY STELA

THEBES SITE No. 14 PLATE XLII

1. OSIRIDE FIGURE

2. MUD FERETORY OR SHRINE

3. REED BURIAL OF A MAN

4. THE UNDER-SIDE OF LID OF A WOODEN BOX WITH INSCRIPTIONS

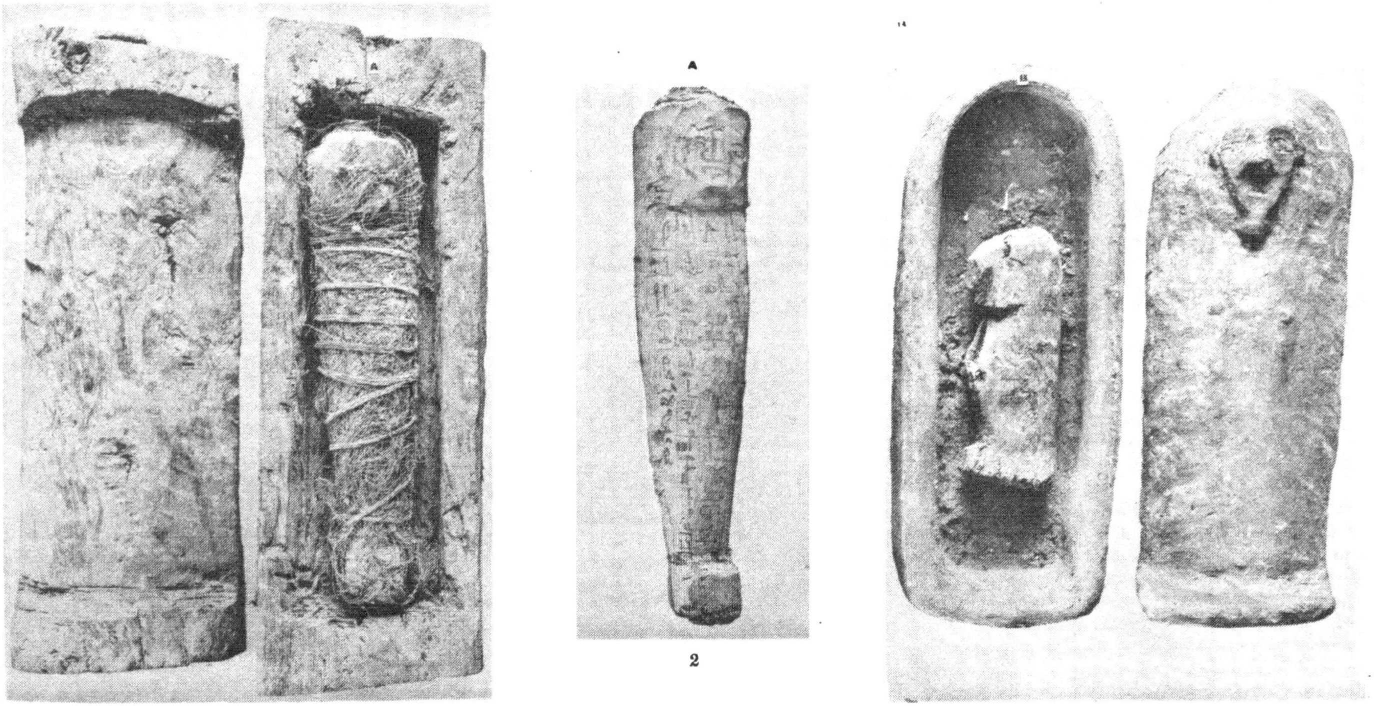

1, 2, & 3. Funerary Statuettes and Model Coffins

Tomb 24

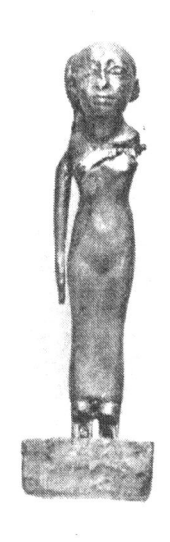

1. Statuette of Ankhu
2. Mummy Decoration 
3. Wooden Doll 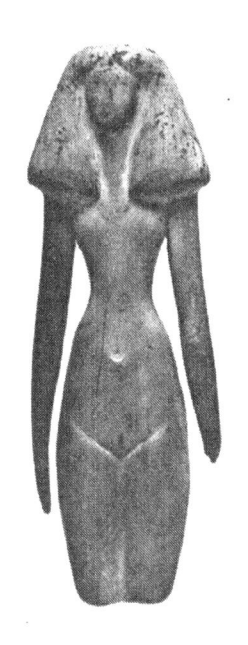
4. Faience Bowl 
5. Faience Bowl

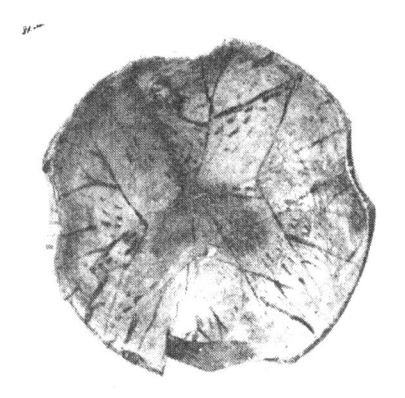

1. Jewel-box

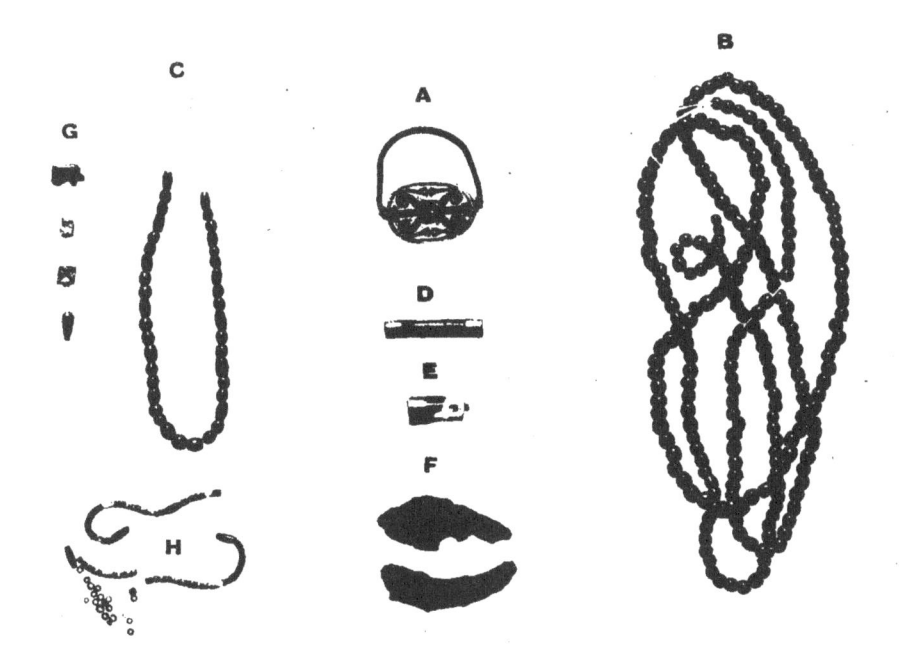

2. Contents of Jewel-box

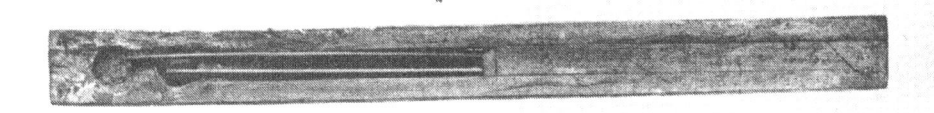

3. Scribe's Palette

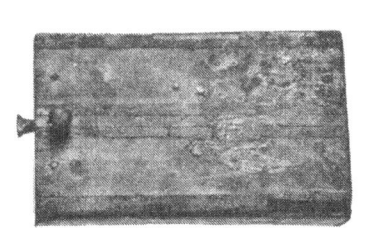

1. Jewel-box

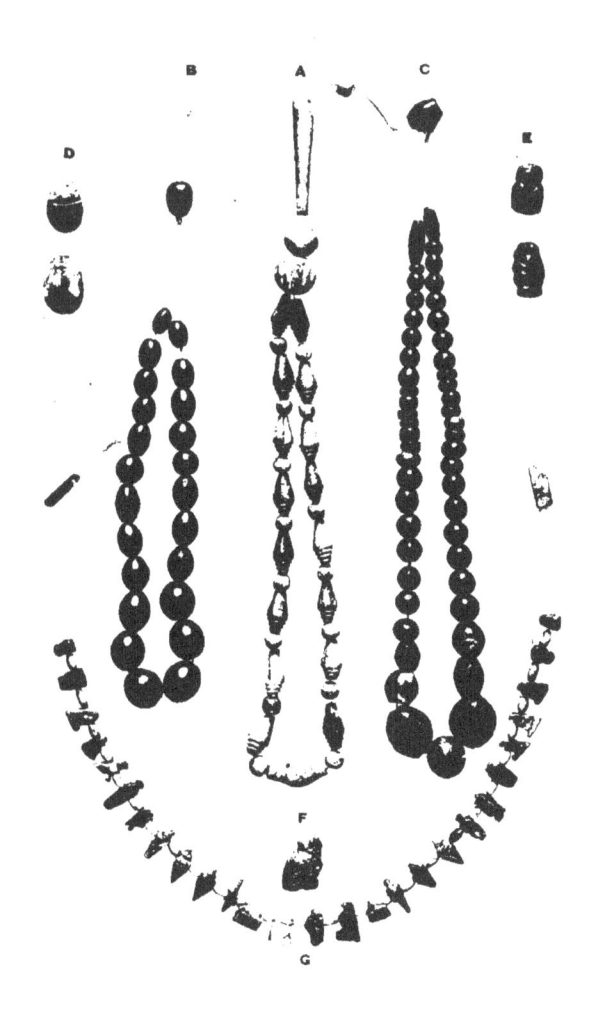

2. Contents of Jewel-box

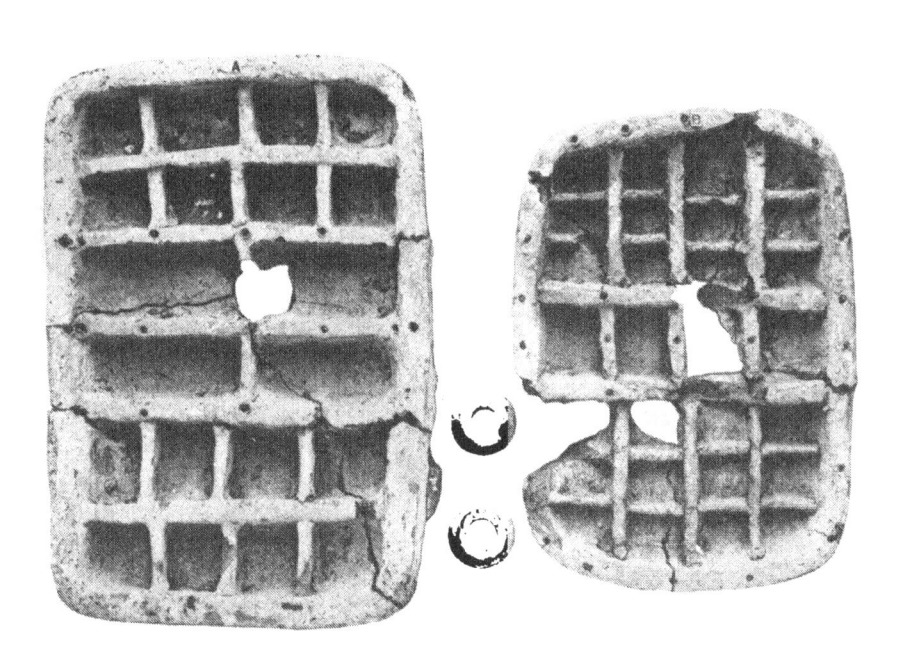

1 & 2. Pottery Vessels and Pans

TOMB 25

1. IVORY AND EBONY TOILET-BOX

2. THE SAME WITH DRAWER AND LID OPEN

Tomb 25

1. Scene engraved on the Front of the Toilet-box

2. Inscriptions on Lid of Toilet-box

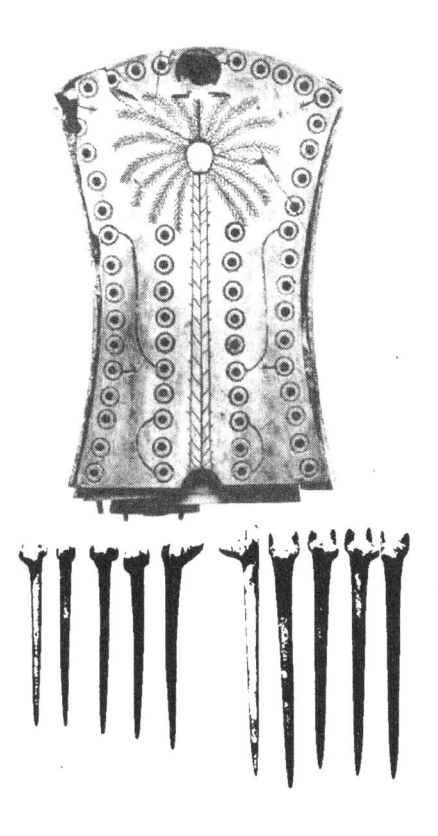

1 & 2. Gaming-Board and Playing Pieces in Ivory

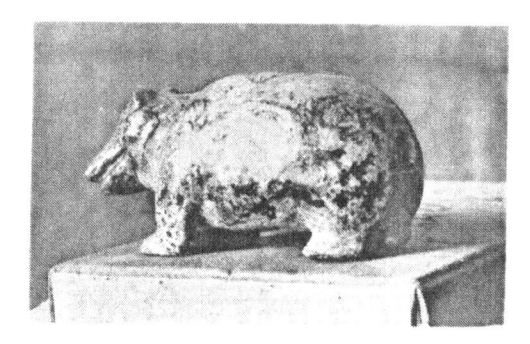

1. Blue Faience Hippopotamus

2. Obsidian and Gold Necklace; Bronze, Ebony and Gold Mirror and 'Shen' Brooch of Cornelian and Gold

Tomb 25

1. Alabaster Vases belonging to the Toilet-box

2. Pottery from Tomb No. 25

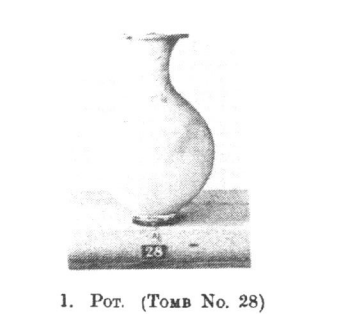

TOMBS 28, 29, 31, 32, 33, 34

1. Pot. (Tomb No. 28)

2. Pottery from Tombs Nos. 31 to 34

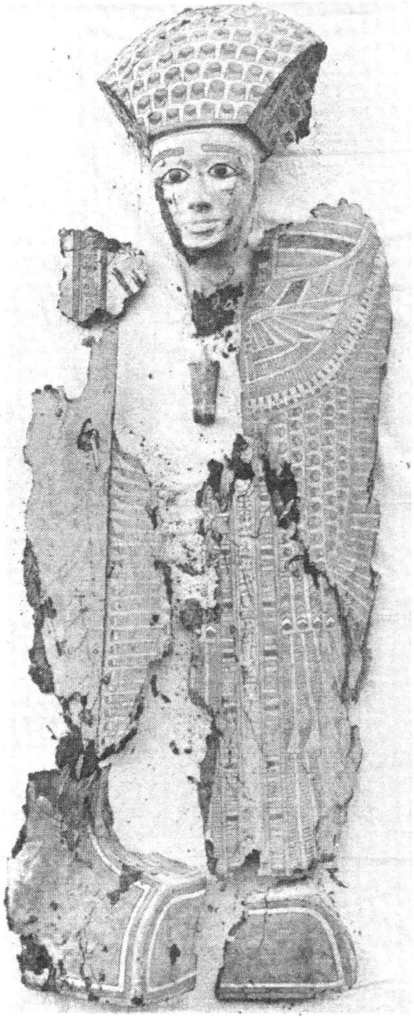

3. Rishi Coffin. (Tomb No. 32)

4. Dug-out Coffins. (Tomb No. 29)

5. Pottery from Tombs Nos. 29, 29 A, and 29 B

STELA OF THE 'KEEPER OF THE BOW' AUY-RES

Tomb 37

North Wing of Corridor showing Closed Doorway of Chamber A

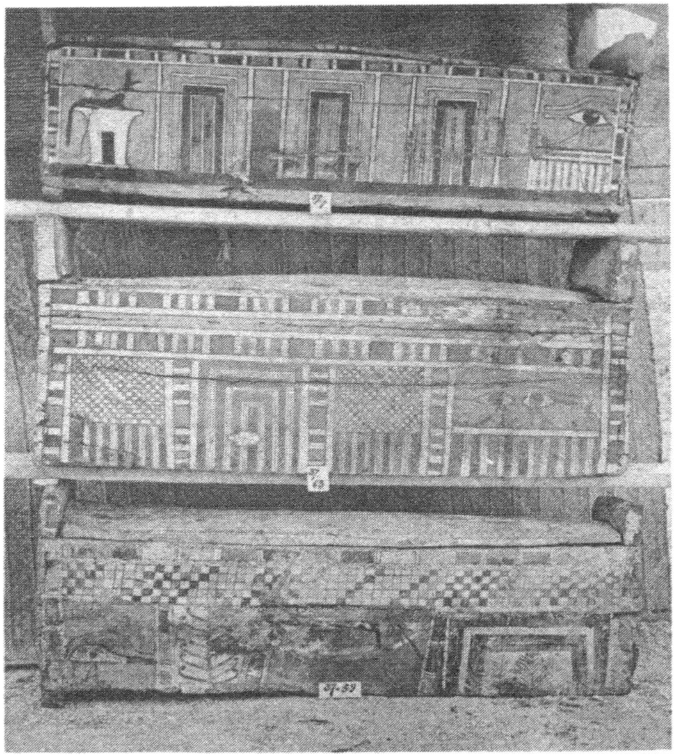

1. Decorated Rectangular Coffins

2. Plain Rectangular Coffins

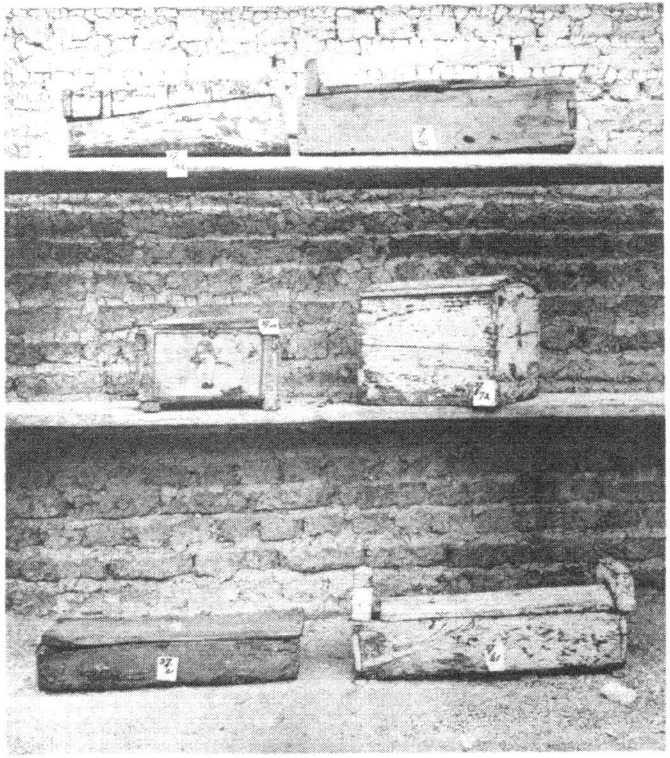

1. CHILDREN'S COFFINS AND VISCERAE BOXES

2. PLAIN ANTHROPOID, 'DUG-OUT' AND SEMI-DECORATED ANTHROPOID COFFINS

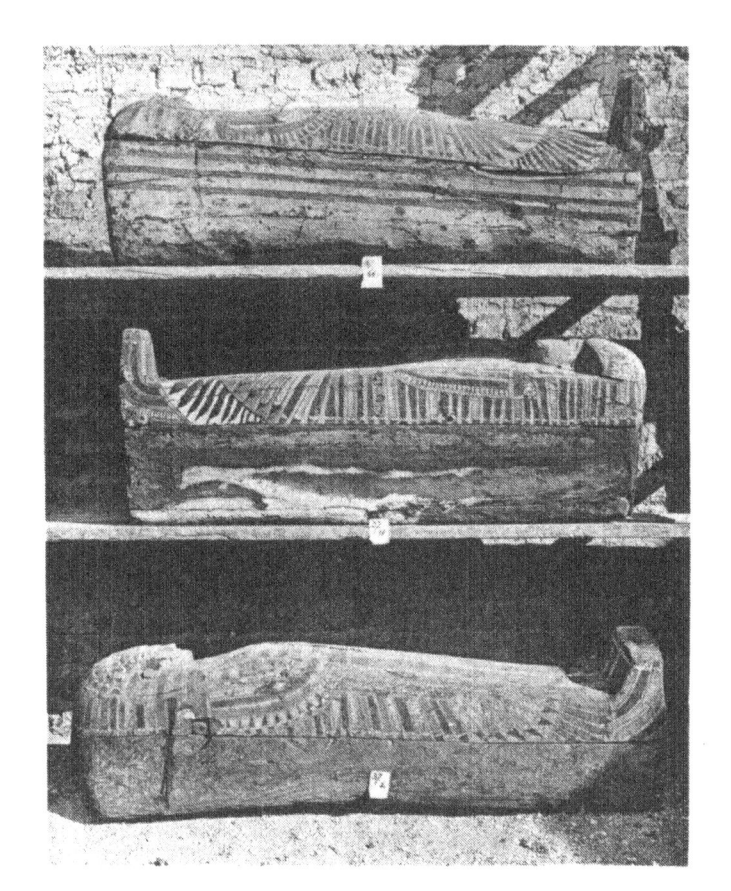

1. Rîshi Coffins

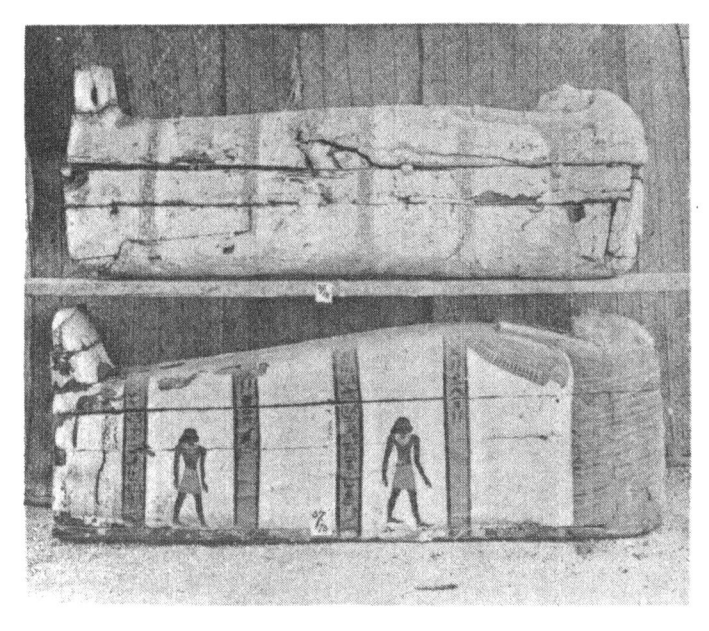

2. Decorated Anthropoid Coffins of the New Empire

THEBES

PLATE LXIII

TOMB 37

DECORATED ANTHROPOID COFFIN OF THE NEW EMPIRE

TOMB 87

1. RUSH-WORK BASKETS

2. MECHANICAL TOY BIRD AND BIRD TRAP

THEBES   PLATE LXV

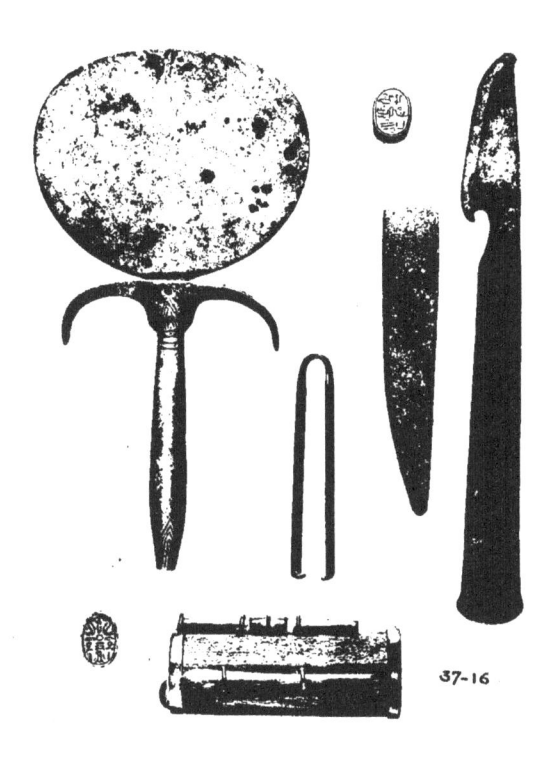

TOMB 37

37-16

1. TOILET SET

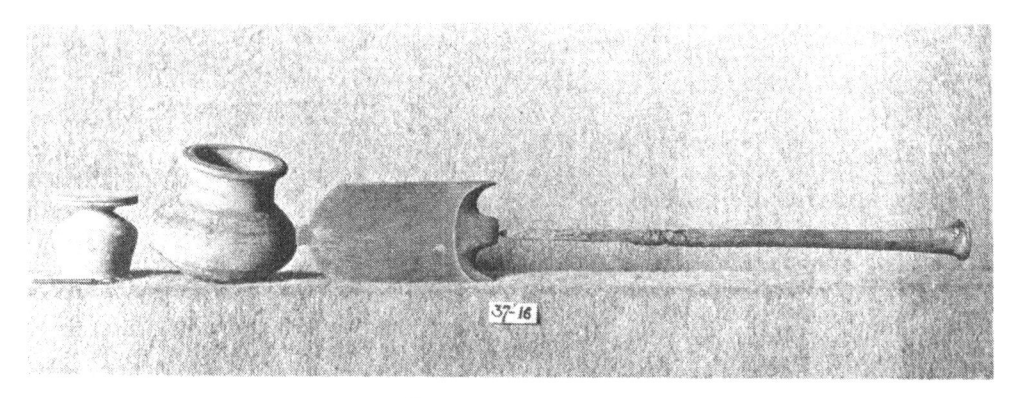

2. FAN-HOLDER, KOHL-POT, &c.

TOMB 37

1. OBJECTS FROM RÎSHI COFFINS

2. OBJECTS FROM RÎSHI COFFINS

THEBES PLATE LXXI

TOMB 37

1. CHAIR AND STOOL

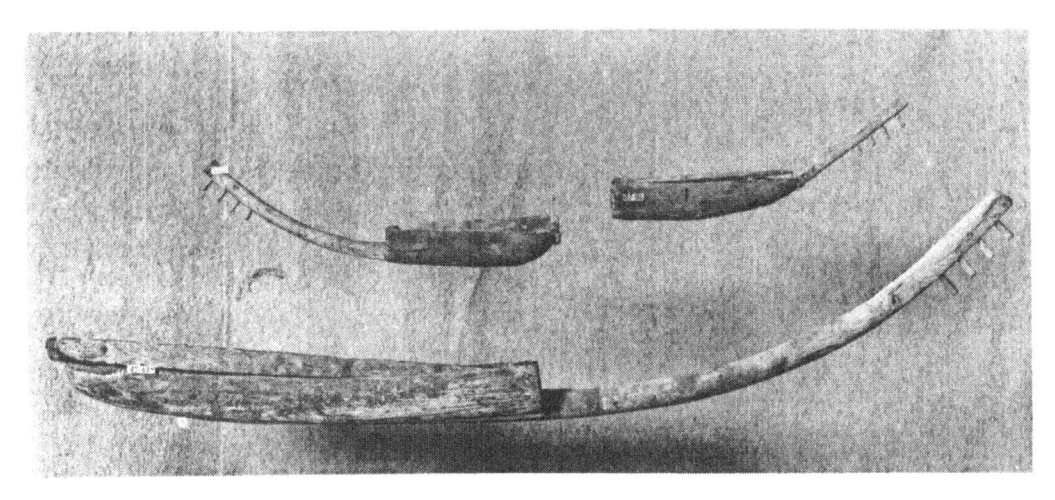

2. MUSICAL INSTRUMENTS

TOMB 37

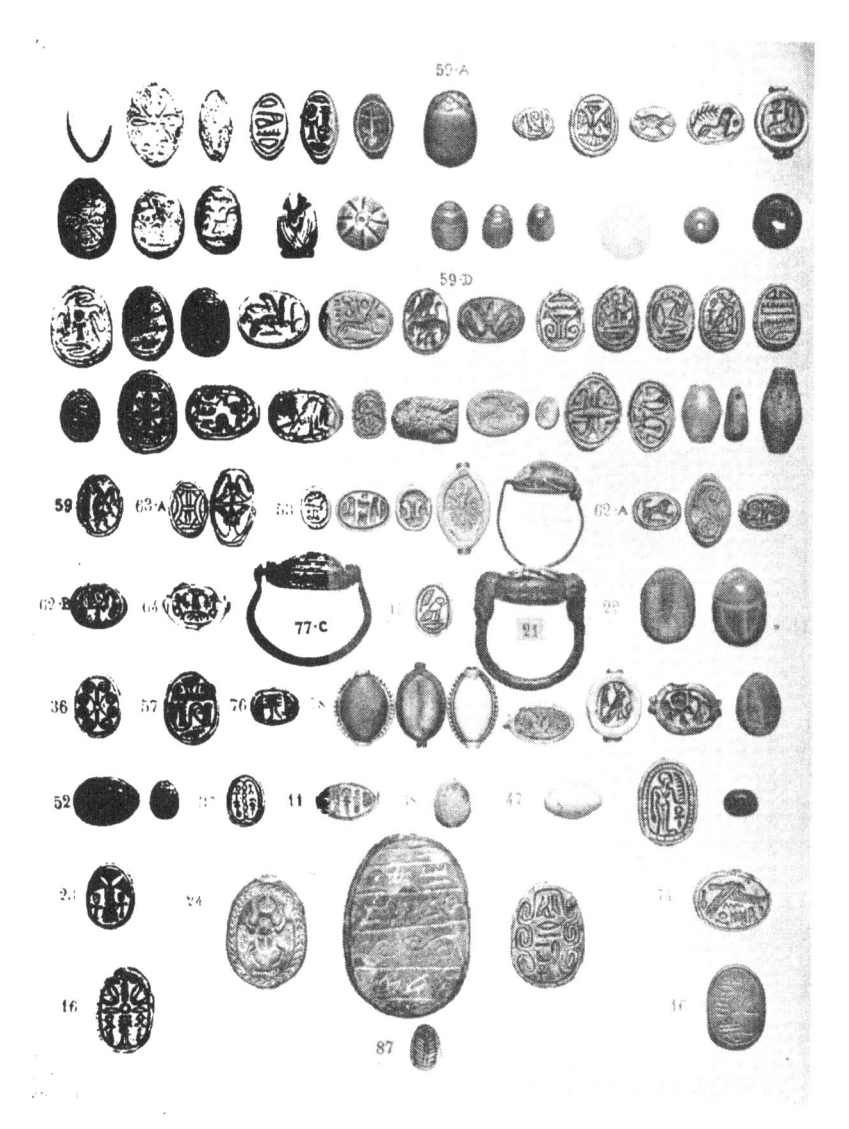

SCARABS, COWROIDS, AND RINGS

THEBES   PLATE LXXIII

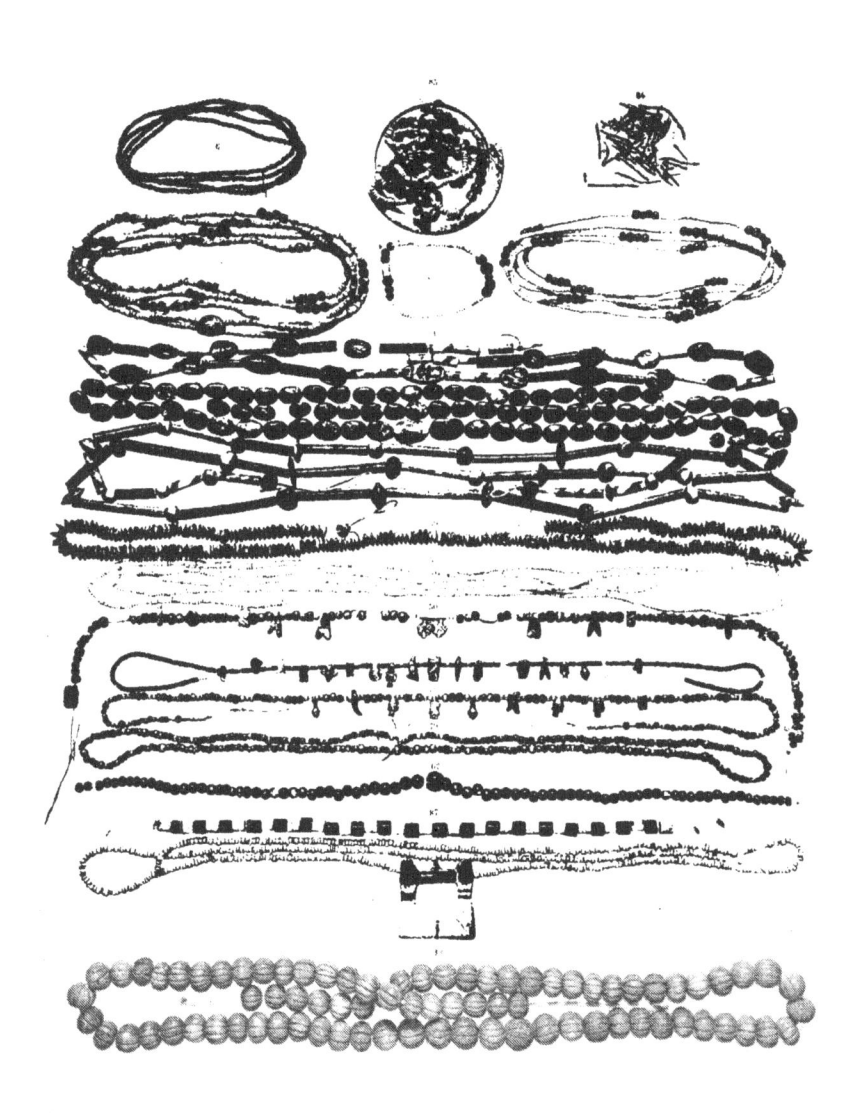

TOMB 37

BEAD NECKLACES, BANGLES, AND BRACELET

THEBES PLATE LXXIV

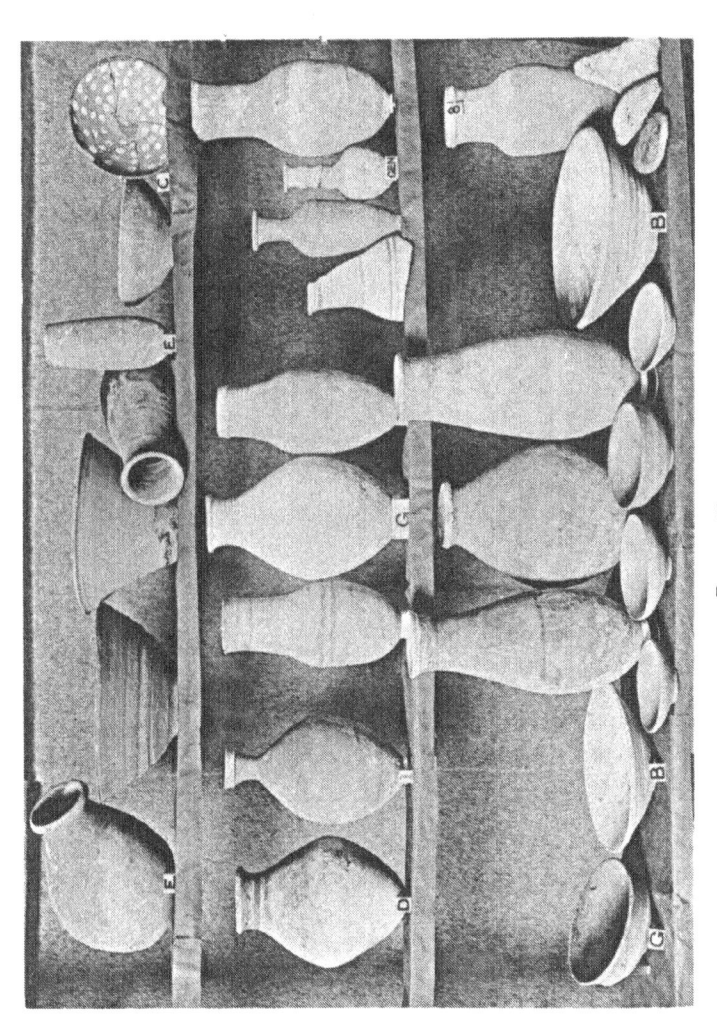

Tomb 37

Pottery Vessels

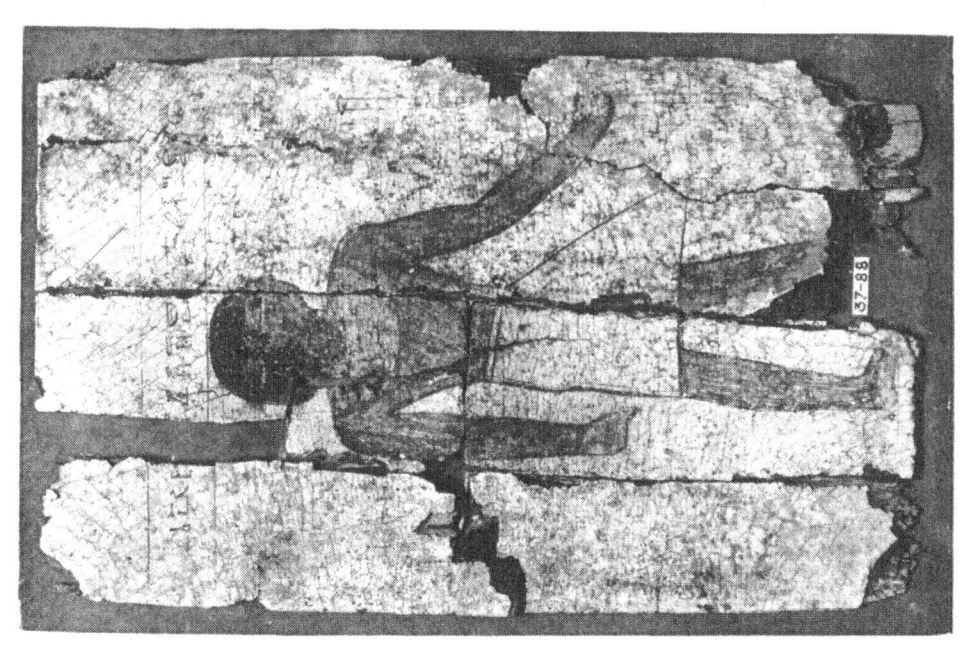

Tomb 37

Panel Stelae

TOMB 37

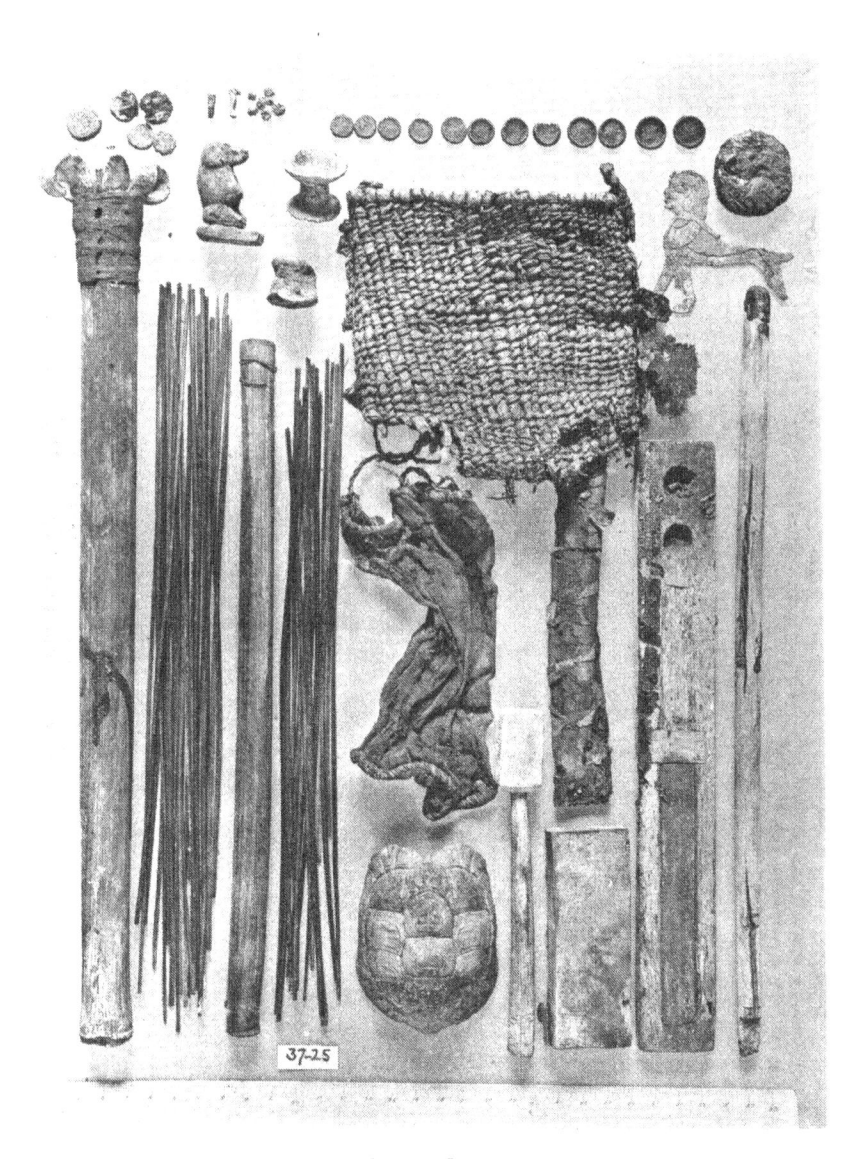

SCRIBE'S OUTFIT

THEBES

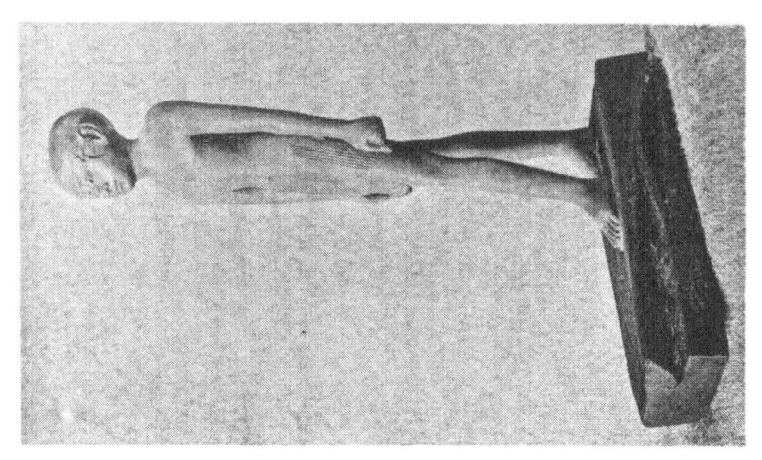

TOMB 37

PLATE LXVII

3. WOODEN STATUETTE

2. STATUETTES LYING IN COFFIN NO. 24

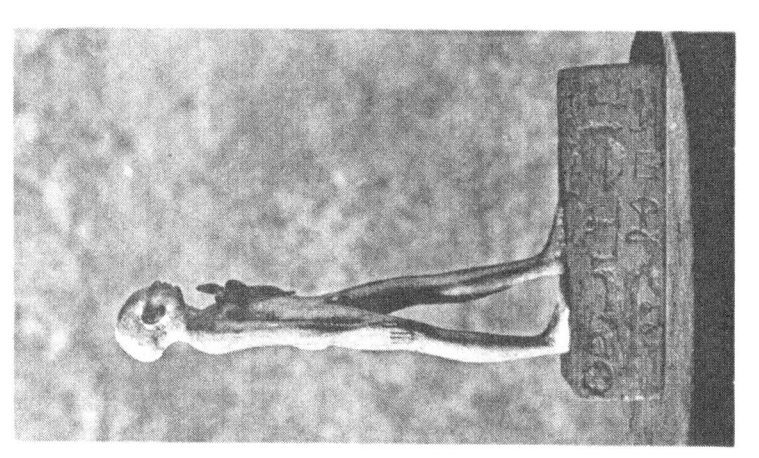

1. ELECTRUM STATUETTE

THEBES PLATE LXIX

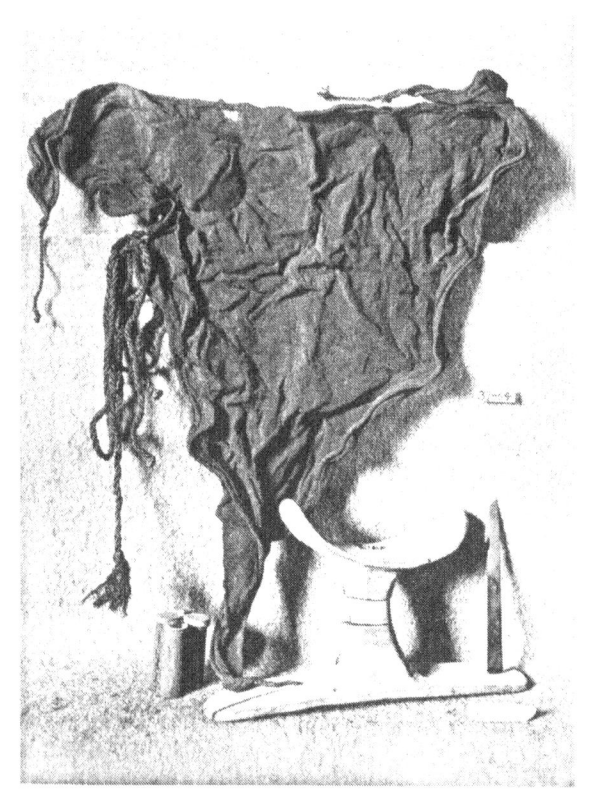

TOMB 37

1. OBJECTS FROM A RECTANGULAR GABLE-TOPPED COFFIN

2. OBJECTS FROM PLAIN RECTANGULAR COFFIN

Томв 37

1. Writing Tablet. No. 28, Rev.

2. Writing Tablet. No. 28, Obv.

1. SEAL IMPRESSIONS ON DOORWAY OF CHAMBER A

2. INTERIOR OF CHAMBER A

TOMB 37

1. CHAMBER B BEFORE OPENING

2. CHAMBER B AFTER OPENING

Томв 37

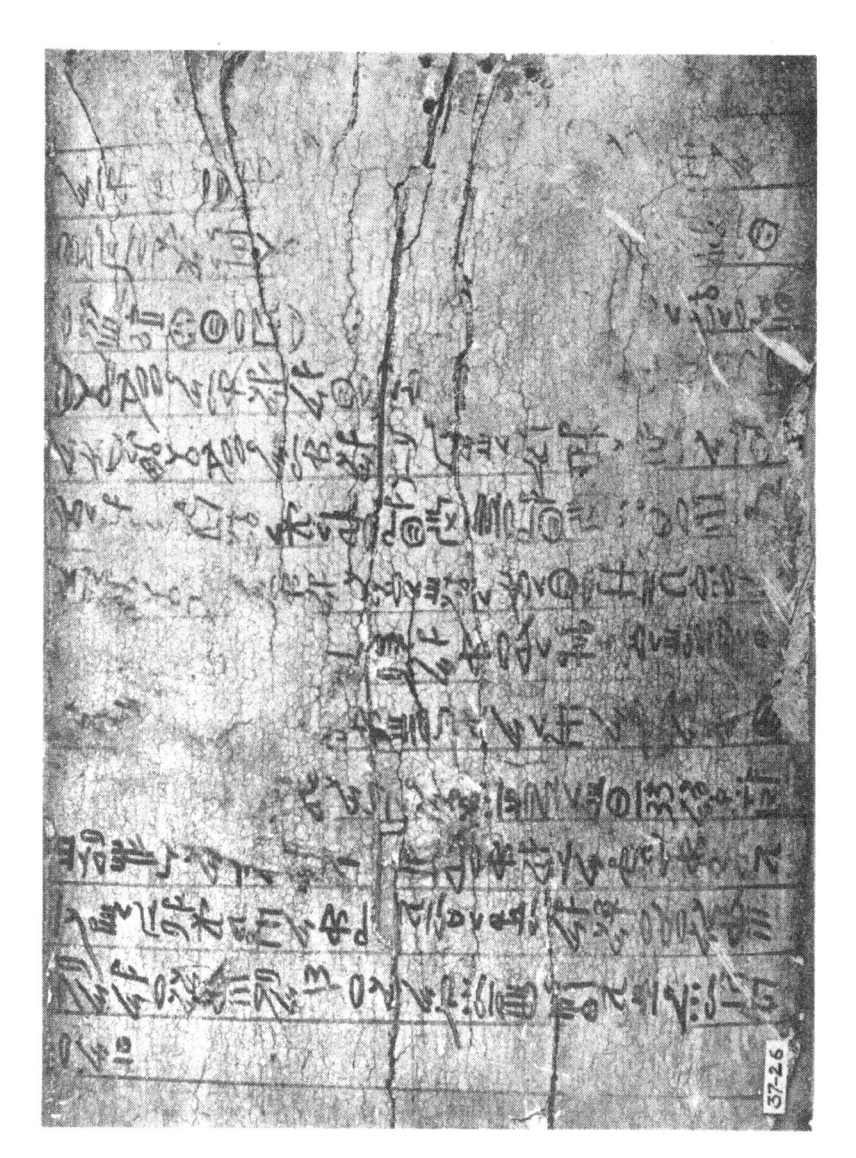

WRITING TABLET. NO. 26, OBV.

THEBES PLATE LXXVIII

TOMB 37

WRITING TABLET. NO. 26, REV.

THEBES   PLATE LV

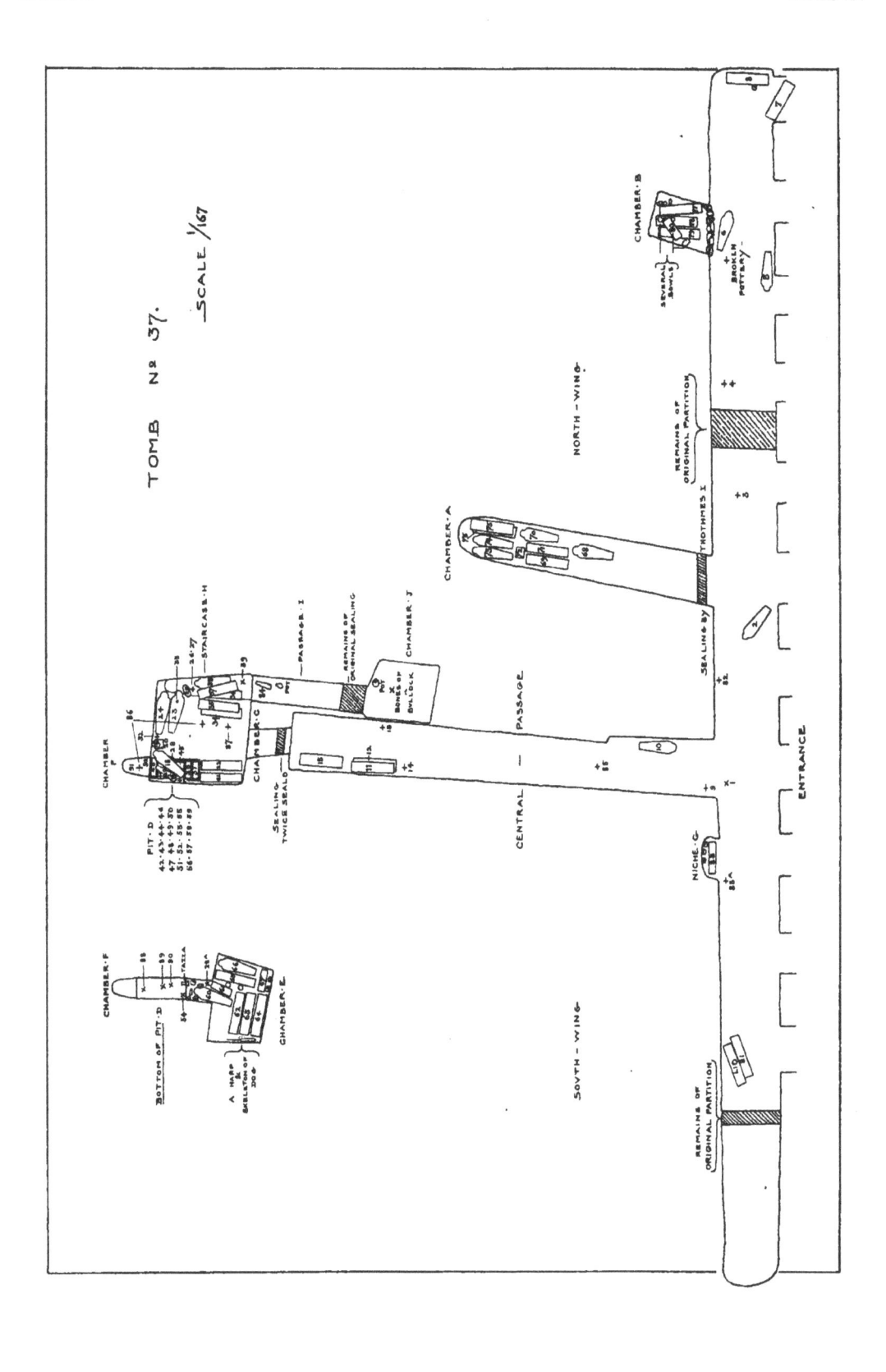

TOMB 37

CENTRAL PASSAGE SHOWING CLOSED DOORWAY OF HALL C

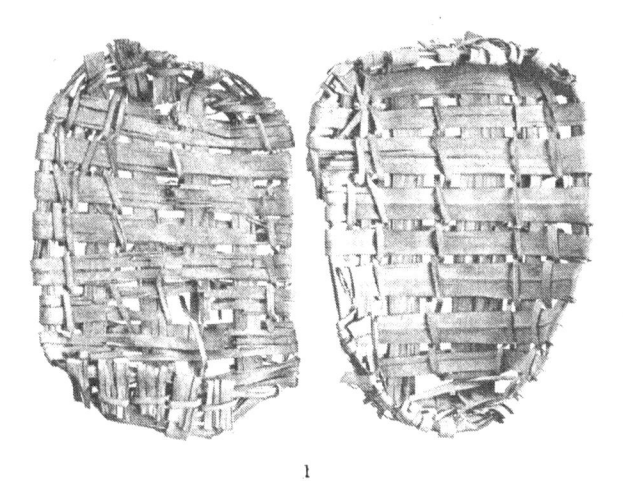

1. FIG BASKETS   2. BOTANICAL SPECIMENS

Tomb 37

1. Objects from Decorated Rectangular Coffins

2. Objects from Plain Rectangular Coffins

32101 075984342